THE CLASSIC ENGLISH GARDENING GUIDES

# FOLIAGE

PLANNING AND PLANTING

THE CLASSIC ENGLISH GARDENING GUIDES

# FOLIAGE

PLANNING AND PLANTING

**ANNA PAVORD**
—— **SERIES EDITOR** ——
**PENELOPE HOBHOUSE**

*1817*

Harper & Row Publishers, Inc. **New York,**
**Grand Rapids, Philadelphia, St. Louis, San Fransisco,**
**London, Singapore, Sydney, Tokyo, Toronto.**

First Published in Great Britain in 1990 by
PAVILION BOOKS LIMITED

Copyright © Anna Pavord

Designed by Elizabeth Ayer

First US edition.

Library of Congress Cataloging-in-Publication Data available upon request.

ISBN 0 06 016527 8

Printed and bound in Italy by New Interlitho, Milan

10   9   8   7   6   5   4   3   2   1

*This book is dedicated to the memory of my parents Grimn and Cristobel Pavord.*

# CONTENTS

# INTRODUCTION

The whole purpose of a flower is to seduce, not only us, but more importantly the creatures that it depends on for pollination and so for survival. Foliage, relieved of this biological imperative, operates in a much more subtle way. You may fall instantly, madly and passionately in love with a flower. An affair with foliage will be cooler, but in the end more sustaining. You do not have to be many seasons into your first garden before you realize that while a flower may be up, out and over in a month, leaves can put up a six- or even a twelve-month show. Of course, the fact that leaves are just *there* does not necessarily make them a pleasure to be with. However you look at it, the foliage of forsythia or philadelphus is undistinguished. There would be no justification for finding either shrub a home in the garden were it not for their flowers. A foliage plant has therefore generally come to mean any plant whose foliage is better than its flowers. Occasionally in this book, you will find plants whose foliage is only as good as their flowers, but no excuses are offered for that little aberration. A realization of its foliage value may persuade you to plant a *Cytisus battandieri*, for instance, which has superb silky grey leaves as well as fine, scented racemes of flowers, rather than a *Solanum jasminoides* 'Album' which, though vogueish, has leaves that are mediocre.

It is not surprising that when one first starts to garden, like a primary schoolchild, one goes for colour. An appreciation of foliage marks the transition to one's secondary education

*Strap-shaped leaves of the hart's tongue fern (*Phyllitis scolopendrium*) and rounded leaves of bergenia soften the outline of the wellhead on the cedar lawn at Tintinhull.*

as a gardener. There is no need to get too precious about all this, to wince at the sight of a large yellow crocus or dive into the hostas when a marigold impinges on the view. There is plenty of room even in the smallest garden for both flowers and foliage. The fun lies in choosing the best combinations, and these of course will change according to the garden's setting. There is a particularly strong case for using plenty of foliage in small, walled town gardens. Here the balance between foliage and flowers might tip strongly in favour of the former. A country garden is made against a background of trees, hedges, fields and sky. The need for a mass of soothing green is less acute than among the hard surfaces of town: tarmac, brick, concrete.

There is another reason, too, why foliage plants work particularly well in town gardens. The formal, architectural quality of plants such as fatsia and fig, bay and bamboo, yucca and yew suits the man-made settings of most town gardens. They become as much sculpture as plant, but sculpture that sometimes has the added dimension of movement, as when bamboo leaves flutter and rustle with the wind. Even if you garden in a courtyard covered with concrete, foliage need not be jettisoned as all the plants mentioned above will grow happily in tubs, provided they are regularly fed and watered. This will give a much lusher, more luxurious effect than if you fill all available pots with petunias. Petunias are pretty things, but they lack bulk, they lack presence. Their leaves do what leaves have to do, but they are unremarkable in form, texture or colour. The plant itself does not have a graceful or dramatic habit of growth. It is always best to treat petunias as trimmings, and let foliage provide the major furnishings.

*Pampas grass* (Cortaderia selloana) *makes a fountain of foliage
at the west end of the terrace at Powis Castle.*

Remember that – except for the greys, which have adapted naturally to hot, dry situations – foliage plants need lush conditions: plenty of water so there is no check to growth and (with one important exception) plenty of nitrogen to feed the leaves. Variegated plants are that exception: they should not be fed too heavily or they will revert to green.

You do not necessarily jettison colour when you go for foliage. Apart from a few isolated specimens such as coleus and tovara, the colour will be muted, but it will be there. A vast array of colours, from the matt, near-black of some conifers to the delicate pale translucence of new beech leaves, are lumped under the name of green. There are purple, gold, blue (or more truthfully bluish), glaucous, grey and truly silver leaves. There is also variegated foliage. Patterns of variegation can be as multifarious as a bird's feathering: striped, blotched, margined, stippled. Leaves may also have one colour on the topside and a different one on the underside, like the white poplar, *Populus alba*, which has deeply lobed leaves, plain grey green on the upper surface, woolly white underneath. Some rhododendrons perform the same double act. In the main rhododendron foliage is glum, but many large-leaved species such as *R. sinograre* and *R. macabeanum* have beautiful leaves, dark green above, thickly felted with white underneath. Others of the family have leaves with undersides covered in warm, russet-coloured moss, properly called indumentum. The *yakushimanum* hybrids are a case in point. Rhododendrons are rarely used primarily as foliage plants, but if you are going to plant one at all, it makes sense to choose one with leaves that can give almost as much pleasure as the flowers.

There is also tremendous variation in the way that plants hold their leaves. The pleasure of looking at trees such as *Populus tremula* or *Tilia* 'Petiolaris' lies not only in their overall shape, but also in the way that the leaves move even in the slightest breeze. If you pick a leaf, you will find that each has a very long stalk or petiole attaching it to the twig and this is why the leaves have such freedom to flutter and dance in the wind.

*The deeply lobed, dark glossy green leaves of an oriental plane* (Platanus orientalis) *at Ascott.*

*Fine foliage in the newly restored conservatory at Wallington. Dramatic fronds of the fern,*
Woodwardia radicans *spill over the front of the staging with feathery stems of tender*
*acacia behind. Regular damping down of the stone floor increases humidity in summer.*

Most of the examples of how to use foliage plants in this book have been taken from National Trust gardens, but plants are not snobs. A fern will grow just as happily in a modern, aluminium, lean-to greenhouse as it does in the grand conservatories at TATTON PARK or BLICKLING. It will mind very much if you let it get too hot or too dry, but it will not miss the finials or the elegant fenestration one little bit. You may not have thirty yards of herbaceous border to play with as Lawrence Johnston did at HIDCOTE, but this should not stop you from trying to put together plants so that they are enhanced rather than engulfed by each other's presence.

Foliage plants have an important part to play in the modern mixed border. They can act as buffers to separate groups of colour that together might be as discordant as a badly tuned piano. Though there are exceptions in all species, many useful border plants – asters, dahlias, members of the daisy family, penstemons – have foliage that is at best undistinguished, at worst downright ragged. Careful placing of foliage plants will disguise these shortcomings very well. They bring an outstanding variety of form to mixed plantings: fat rounded leaves of bergenia, feathery plumes of artemisia, stiff sword shapes of phormium and yucca.

*Ferns and low growing ground cover plants line the steps down to the well garden at Acorn Bank. The bronze purple foliage of a cotinus, here softened by the fuzz of its smoky flowers provides an excellent colour contrast with the bright yellow green of the ferns.*

*The open fronted arcade on the aviary terrace at Powis Castle provides shelter for tender, scented rhododendrons such as 'Lady Alice Fitzwilliam'. A small-leaved variegated ivy disguises the front of the raised brick bed and the evergreen* Ficus pumila, *more commonly seen as a houseplant, is trained up the arch.*

Low-growing foliage plants are particularly useful for softening areas of paving or steps. In old terraces, there are usually enough cracks and holes to push plants into (and many will seed themselves there). In new paving you may have to steel yourself to chip a corner off a paving slab to make a suitable home. Though this may seem like desecration, the effect will be well worth it. Plant the pretty New Zealand burr, either *Acaena* 'Blue Haze' with fine, filigree pewter-coloured leaves, or the bronze-coloured *A. microphylla*, and there will be no question in your mind that this is

a great deal easier on the eye than an unrelieved mass of sterile slabs. Bugle, variegated arabis and the purple-leaved *Viola labradorica* will be equally happy in a position like this, where, even if their heads are in the sun, their roots will be in the cool, moist soil under the slabs.

*Foliage plants make useful permanent features in urns and tubs. A formal, clipped ball of box complements a fine urn at Ascott.*

*The symmetrical forms of sempervivums provide year-round interest in foreground plantings. All this family thrive in sun and when planted in shallow earthenware pots.*

Foliage plants are invaluable allies when it comes to planting up pots. Shrubs can be planted one to a big pot; low spreading Japanese maples look particularly good in the plain blue-glazed pots imported from China. Aralia will also thrive in a large tub and provide a bold foliage background for smaller containers of bulbs or annuals. Small sedums, saxifrages and sempervivums, which make neat rosettes of leaves, can be grown separately in shallow terracotta pans. Mixed plantings are more difficult to bring off successfully, but at the same time, more exciting when they do succeed. If they do not, it should not be the occasion for much beating of the breast. There is always another season. *Helichrysum petiolare* (formerly *H. petiolatum*) is one of the most useful of all foliage plants for what used to be called pot-work. It is not hardy, but this need not matter if you have the wherewithal either to buy fresh plants each April or May or to take cuttings and overwinter them inside in a greenhouse or on the kitchen windowsill. The plant grows in a rambling way and has white felted leaves, heart-shaped, but no more than 25mm/1in long. It is not a swamper, but threads itself about very elegantly among neighbours.

Ivy is another stalwart of tubs and has the advantage of being evergreen and hardy. *Hedera helix* 'Abundance', *H.h.* 'Glache' and *H.h.* 'Heise' are particularly good trailing varieties. In spring they give substance to plantings of tulips and daffodils. In summer they cool down a display of lilies. In winter they can hold the fort alone.

Ivy is also one of the most common foliage plants to be used on walls. The large-leaved 'Sulphur Heart' (syn. 'Paddy's Pride') is one of the most popular, but small-leaved varieties can be used equally effectively. 'Sulphur Heart' can be overpowering in quantity. The leaves are *too* large, coarse and shapeless and the variegation is a particularly virulent combination of sulphurous yellow and pale green. At BLICKLING, big arched niches in a brick wall are filled with the small yellow-leaved ivy 'Buttercup'. This shines out against the brickwork and accentuates the architectural outline of the arches. You can get a similar effect on a plain wall, even a hideous breeze-block one, by growing ivy over it, later clipping away growth to leave clean arch shapes of masonry behind. You can then use the plain flat arches framed in green to display a piece of sculpture or a massed collection of pots raised on a semicircular stand.

In the garden at Lamport Hall, Northamptonshire, ivy was used in the nineteenth century to make a green background for other climbers trained on the walls. The ivy clung to the wall itself, roses and clematis were tied in front of the ivy on wires held at least 150mm/6in out from the face of the wall by long-necked vine eyes. This sort of double banking of climbers needs vigilance, for tendrils of ivy will always be ready to creep out and strangle less vigorous companions. The effect would be lush and splendid, but a plain ivy in this

*Lush foliage of parthenocissus softens the gaunt stonework of the pele tower at Sizergh Castle. Choose varieties with care. Some are too vigorous for all but the largest sites.*

*Gunnera is perhaps the most dramatic foliage plant that can be grown in Britain. Certainly it is the largest. It is slightly tender and thrives best where it has plenty of moisture.*

situation would be less distracting than a variegated one. One of the less invasive parthenocissus such as *P. henryana* could be used in the same way though it is not evergreen. The more rampant creepers – either the true Virginia creeper, *P. quinquefolia*, or the Boston ivy, *P. tricuspidata* – need to be used with care. They clothe areas very quickly, which may be what you think you want, but after two years' pleasure, there will be endless years of pain, wobbling on top of a ladder preventing the thing from entirely blocking the gutters, from getting under the roof and from obscuring windows. *P. tricuspidata*, though it has the best autumn colour, is particularly wicked in this respect. *P. henryana* is much more manageable and – though it does not colour quite as brilliantly in autumn – has leaves that are generally more handsome, dark, velvety green marked with pink and white along the midrib and veins.

Foliage and water are as naturally companionable as sea

and sand, and the rule here is to adjust the scale of the one to suit the other. In the Trust's gardens, the scale is often very large indeed and giant gunnera (*G. manicata*) – with leaves large enough to picnic under in a rainstorm – seem entirely appropriate. Though coarse performers when seen in close-up, viewed from a proper distance these massive foliage plants make an arresting display. Their leaves are the biggest of any plant that we can grow outdoors in Britain and, when suited, can stretch up to 3m/10ft across. Gunnera is slightly tender and will not be happy unless it has plenty of moisture. For planting on a more domestic scale by a pool or stream, rheum is easier to manage, either the purple-tinged *R. palmatum* or its truly purple cultivar *R.p.* 'Atrosanguineum'. In the average back garden, rodgersia will be the best choice of all. It is built to an easier scale and is no less handsome. Rather than the rhubarb-leaves of the other two, most rodgersias have leaves like a horse chestnut's, but richly tinted with bronze at the beginning of the season. *R. tabularis* (now correctly *Astilboides t.*) is slightly different with large, soft scalloped leaves like a frilly tablecloth. By nature, these are plants of damp bog, but *R. podophylla* will tolerate dryer situations. Use them with the handsome thin sword-leaves of acorus, boldly striped in cream and green in the variety *A. calamus* 'Variegatus', or with *Iris pseudacorus* 'Variegata'.

Without such fanciful accessories as petals, bracts, calyx, stigma and stamens to dress in, the overall appearance of a leaf will never be as exotic as that of a flower. A flower is three-dimensional; leaves, being so very thin, are practically two-dimensional. This is not a drawback but means that leaves can be used in a different way from flowers. Sometimes they may stand like black paper silhouettes boldly against the sky. Ivy grown flat on a wall makes intricate, angular patterns, a screen print of green on grey. Creeping Jenny (*Lysimachia nummularia*) between paving slabs makes a similarly flat pattern, but in a different plane. Sometimes leaves may be massed together indistinguishably to make one solid three-dimensional building block in the grander garden design.

*Hundreds of years growth are necessary to make shapes as arresting as these domed bulwarks of yew in front of Powis Castle. At a distance, individual leaflets of yew fuse to make one solid, matt-textured screen of green, imposing in itself, but also an excellent background for the more complicated textures and forms of the plantings in front.*

The evergreens – box, cypress, holly, ilex, yew – can all be used in this way and for low hedges, alongside paths perhaps, so can artemisia, lavender, rosemary or santolina. In a flat garden, hedges provide an important vertical dimension, as well as dividing up space to give some element of secrecy and surprise. The advantage of using evergreens becomes obvious in winter, when, all trimmings stripped away, dark green bulwarks of yew and ilex assume extra importance. In the famous east garden at Hatfield House, Hertfordshire, the parterres are filled all summer with colour and turbulence. In the winter, the emphasis changes and the most important features are the twin avenues of ilex (*Quercus ilex*) on either side of the parterre: tall clean trunks with dark heads of foliage, neatly clipped into balls. A hedge also carries out the same function as a picture frame, focusing the eye on what lies within its boundaries. In this way, a herbaceous border viewed against a busy background will be less effective than one contained and displayed in front of a plain, dark evergreen hedge.

Yew, or rather a pair of yews, can also be used as sentries to guard an entrance or signal a grand view. They are used in this way on either side of the parterres at ASHDOWN HOUSE. If you cannot wait for yew, use groups of dramatic foliage plants such as phormium or acanthus. They work like punctuation marks, inviting you to pause, to exclaim, marking the beginning or the end of a garden statement.

Foliage plants give bulk and shape to a garden. If you are feeling dissatisfied with the view over your own patch, it could well be that you have underestimated the need for foliage in the garden: some stands of biennial angelica or perennial bamboo to give substance and drama to what might otherwise be an over-fussy assemblage of plants chosen for their flowers alone; cool pools of plain round-leaved hostas or bergenias to soothe senses jaded by extravagant colour; a stretch of smooth grass or a plain bulwark of clipped Portugal laurel to separate areas of great busyness; evergreens to give winter bones and sustenance when flowers are at their nadir.

*Viewed in close-up, yew becomes a different plant. The mass separates into a myriad of tiny narrow leaves, here on a golden form of the common yew,* Taxus baccata *at Ascott.*

# FORM

The shape of a leaf is its most variable characteristic. Learning how to manipulate this diversity is one of the fundamental lessons of gardening, but it is all rather more complicated than painting by numbers. Plants are living creatures, not designer toys. They have developed an infinite variety of form for their convenience and better survival, not solely for our pleasure. Le Corbusier did not invent the theory of form and function. Plants have known it, and have been practising it, forever. The function of a leaf is to capture light for photosynthesis. Its form, essentially thin and flat, has developed a myriad variations to ensure that this happens in the most efficient way.

Our gain lies in the results of this profligate adaptation: the solid, sword-like foliage of iris and phormium, the hand-shaped leaves of rodgersia or horse chestnut, the filmy, thread-like haze of fennel, intricate parallel fronds of fern, arum leaves like arrows. Both William Robinson and Gertrude Jekyll recognized that this diversity of form was an attribute every bit as important as colour. Constance Spry, doyenne of flower arrangers, brought the message to a wider audience. In *The Garden Notebook* published in 1940 she wrote, 'The beauty of a border lies not only in the colour grouping but also in the clever juxtaposition of contrasting shapes. Plants of one type, habit and form of foliage look well set next to strongly contrasting forms; a vigorous leaf by a filmy one, a slender spire by a massive head. This contributes to the general effect.'

*The tender Chatham Island forget-me-not (Myosotidium hortensia) is not an easy plant to grow well, but has handsome prominently ribbed leaves of glossy green.*

*Deeply cut leaves, such as are found on acers, parthenocissus and Boston ivy are amongst the most handsome of foliage forms.*

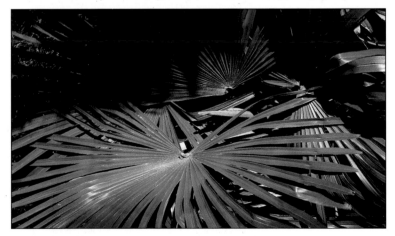

*Palms such as this Chusan or fan palm (Trachycarpus fortunei) will not thrive in cold areas. The crisply pleated leaves up to 900mm/3ft wide are borne on sharply toothed stalks.*

Leaf shape – pinnate, palmate or any other '-ate' that fevered botanists may decide on – is only one aspect of plant form. There is also the question of a plant's overall shape and size, its stature. Angelica has a particularly statuesque quality. It is a plant that you use for its overall effect, rather than for its particular leaf, though these are handsome enough, particularly in early spring when they push through the ground with immense lushness. If you break a stem, it immediately releases the spicy smell of cake shops and Christmas. The plant is an exercise in monochrome: green stems, green flowers and leaves, though there is a hint of pink in the stems sometimes and the great globe of flowers tends towards a creamier green than the leaves. What it has is bulk, presence and an arresting outline. Leaves that first emerge in March will still be shouting for attention in June, but after flowering the leaves lose their healthy sheen and the beauty veers towards the beast. At the opposite end of the scale is *Cotoneaster horizontalis*, which has tiny leaves, each no bigger than a ladybird, but the way that the plant grows, the effect of the mass, with branches held as stiffly as a kipper's backbone, is what really matters in a mixed planting scheme.

## A NORTH-FACING BORDER AT BARRINGTON

Foliage will often be more effective than flowers in traditionally 'difficult' areas of the garden: in the dry shade under trees; in the kind of dark, dank conditions you find at the foot of a north wall. At BARRINGTON COURT Head Gardener Mrs Christine Brain has used just such a position – a long narrow north-facing border under a 2.1m/7ft high stone wall – to demonstrate that foliage plants, well chosen and well contrasted, can make an extremely handsome and long-lasting feature in a garden. The border, punctuated at intervals by the stone pillars of a pergola, is only 1.8m/6ft wide but 30.4m/108ft long, broken in the middle by an archway through into the white garden. The three stalwarts of the planting are all plants which represent fine examples of form: hellebores for winter and early spring, followed by

*The tiny leaves of* Cotoneaster horizontalis, *almost smothered by autumn berries, sit stiffly either side of rigidly held branches. Here the effect of the whole is what matters.*

euphorbias which carry through till early summer when hostas pick up the baton.

She uses three different hellebores: *H. orientalis*, with handsome hand-shaped leaves which push through on stiff strong stems after the flush of winter flowers; *H. argutifolius* (syn. *H. corsicus*), with a three-lobed leaf, edged all round with mock prickles; and *H. lividus*. A variegated evergreen

## BARRINGTON COURT
### Border under north wall

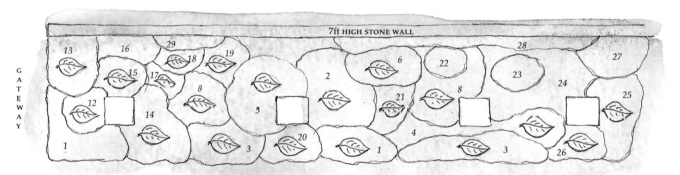

*East Border*

Pergola Pillars

*West Border*

N

1. *Alchemilla mollis*
2. *Hosta sieboldii*
3. *Euphorbia polychroma*
4. *Melissa officinalis* 'Variegata'
5. *Polygonatum multiflorum*
6. *Helleborus orientalis*
7. *Tellima grandiflora*
8. *Hosta* 'Thomas Hogg'
9. *Helleborus lividus corsicus*
10. *Daphne laureola*
11. *Erysimum*

12. *Hosta fortunei* 'Aureomarginata'
13. *Pulmonaria saccharata*
14. *Heuchera* 'Coral Bells'
15. *Helleborus lividus*
16. *Trollius europaeus*
17. Epimedium
18. *Kirengeshoma palmata*
19. *Euphorbia griffithii* 'Fireglow'
20. *Euphorbia cyparissias*
21. *Dicentra spectabilis*
22. *Digitalis purpurea alba*

23. *Paeonia suffruticosa*
24. *Astrantia maxima*
25. *Daphne odora* 'Aureo-marginata'
26. *Nepeta mussinii*
27. *Liatris pycnostachya*
28. *Campsis radicans*
29. *Chaenomeles speciosa* 'Moerloosei'
30. *Cotoneaster horizontalis*
31. *Cotoneaster simonsii*

DIMENSIONS: *1.8m×16.4m (6ft×54ft) for each border*

 FOLIAGE PLANTS

*Luxuriant mounds of foliage plants furnish a potentially difficult area at the foot of a north wall at Barrington Court. Clematis and vines clothe the pergola while the mainstays of the border are hellebores, euphorbias and hostas, particularly the glaucous-leaved* Hosta sieboldiana.

shrub, *Daphne odora* 'Aureomarginata', provides sweet-smelling small flowers at a time when you most need that kind of uplift and a steady framework of good, glossy foliage for the rest of the year. The hellebores, too, are evergreen, though in a different way. New shoots thrust up each year, but the old stems need not be cut away until the new are established. The plant never leaves a gap like most herbaceous perennials.

*Daphne luureola*, a native woodlander, is similarly evergreen and is planted together with *H. argutifolius* on the left-hand side of the door through the wall. It has plain shiny leaves, long and pointed. It is not showy, but handsome, a city-suited shrub, restrained and reliable. Hairy-leaved *Pulmonaria saccharata* fills in a corner on the other side of the doorway and completes the winter planting. Although the pulmonaria flowers at the beginning of the year, its leaves are at their best when flowering is over. They stand firm and, with their hairy texture, seem mercifully unpalatable to slugs. *P. longifolia* is a good form with narrower leaves than the ordinary type and piercingly blue flowers.

Euphorbias are the mainstay of this border in spring. Large clumps of *E. polychroma* sit at intervals along the front of the whole border, vivid acid yellow when in flower, a good mound of light oblong leaves when the flowers have faded. In autumn the foliage has pronounced bronze tints. *E. griffithii* 'Fireglow' flowers at much the same time, but with bracts that are brick red in colour. The leaves are stiff and, though overall olive-green, have shades of purple about them and a curious silvery sheen. This spurge spreads by underground shoots and will quickly make clumps in well-drained, well-fed soil. In the middle of both halves of the border is a bold group of Solomon's seal (*Polygonatum multiflorum*), lovely when hung with its creamy bells in mid-spring, but graceful without, too. The leaves are arranged alternately along arching stems, the veins on each leaf running longitudinally from tip to stalk, to give each one a pleated appearance. Low mounds of bronze-tinted tellima and handsome epimedium are also features in spring.

Hostas at Barrington grow leaves as big as tablemats. Variegated kinds are well used to lighten this dark, sunless strip, but the huge rounded and veined leaves of *H. sieboldiana*, glaucous blue and at least 300mm/1ft long and wide, are perhaps the most arresting. In this planting they contrast well with the thin lance-shaped leaves of *Euphorbia polychroma* and the delicate sprays of Solomon's seal. *Hosta* 'Thomas Hogg' has smaller leaves but is a neat performer, with fresh green pointed leaves, each one edged with cream. It provides a solid background for the feathery foliage of a bleeding heart (*Dicentra spectabilis*). *Hosta fortunei* 'Aureomarginata' has a pronounced yellow band round the leaves and is used in this border with alchemilla either side of the doorway. A couple of clumps of variegated balm (*Melissa officinalis* 'Aurea') shine out and, if cut down at the beginning of June as it begins to produce flower-spikes, will produce a fresh crop of leaves to carry through the rest of the season. This planting scheme could be translated to any equally sunless strip, though attention to feeding will be vital if you want the same lush growth.

*Solid leaves of hosta contrast with the filmy fronds of fern on the edge of the lake at Stourhead. Both enjoy the same rich, damp growing conditions.*

## EMPHATIC SWORD-SHAPED LEAVES

Sword-shaped leaves are immediately arresting, but mostly belong to plants that live in sunny climates. If you have a sheltered garden or are prepared to be sanguine about winter losses, phormiums are superb foliage plants, dramatic punctuation marks among the gentle rounded shapes typical of herbaceous border plants. New Zealand flax (*Phormium tenax*) is an Australasian and needs sun. Most of the new varieties stop at about 900mm/3ft, whereas *P. tenax* 'Purpureum', one of the original introductions, can make 1.8m/6ft of growth and be rather overpowering. Straw or bracken packed loosely around plants will give a modicum of winter protection.

The best use of phormiums in Trust gardens is undoubtedly at OVERBECKS near Salcombe in Devon, where Head Gardener Mr Tony Murdoch shows flashes of pure genius in the way that he puts plants together. Salcombe, on the south-west coast, is a balmy bit of England, however. If you live in Salford in the north-west you may not find it so easy to obtain these Mediterranean effects. In town gardens

*A late summer scene at Overbecks in Devon, where New Zealand flaxes, spiky astelias, cannas, cordylines and yuccas provide strong foliage shapes among softer mounds of flowers. The sword-shaped leaves of the flaxes, mostly varieties of* Phormium cookianum *look equally good in tubs in town gardens.*

## OVERBECKS SALCOMBE
Border beside main path

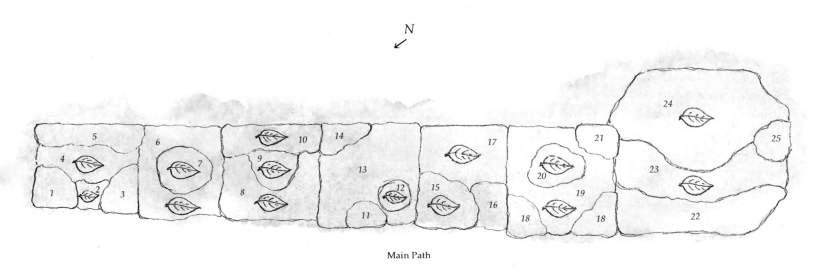

N

Main Path

1. Osteospermum
2. *Yucca whipplei*
3. Osteospermum
4. *Argyranthemum foeniculaceum* 'Chelsea Girl'
5. *Osteospermum ecklonis*
6. *Phormium* 'Cream Delight'
7. *Phormium* 'Bronze Baby'
8. *Astelia chathamica* 'Silver Spear'
9. *Cordyline australis purpurea*
10. *Canna indica* 'Purpurea'
11. *Osteospermum* 'Buttermilk'
12. *Olearia semidentata*
13. *Felicia amelloides*
14. Callistemon
15. *Kniphofia thomsonii snowdenii*
16. *Osteospermum* 'Whirligig'
17. *Argyranthemum foeniculaceum*
18. *Gazania splendens*
19. *Pittosporum* 'Tom Thumb'
20. *Pittosporum* 'Silver Queen'
21. *Lonicera etrusca*
22. Gazania
23. *Phormium purpureum*
24. *Phormium* 'Veitchii'
25. *Lonicera* 'Dropmore Scarlet'

*DIMENSIONS: 5.5m×17.5m (18ft×57ft)*

with favourable microclimates they will look splendidly theatrical. At Overbecks you can see *P. tenax* 'Firebird' with lustrous dark canna lilies and the dark red spiky foliage of *P. cookianum* 'Dazzler' paired with the pale green foliage of *Fuchsia* 'Sharpitor'. The bronze-leaved *Phormium* 'Sundowner' is used in a particularly exotic planting with canna, *Yucca recurvifolia* 'Variegata', darkly mottled silybum which grows wild among the rocks of southern Turkey and the bright flowers of the dahlia 'Redskin'. Yet another New Zealand native used at Overbecks is astelia, similarly spiky but more grassy than the phormiums. *Astelia nivicola* 'Red Gem' makes a neat dome of foliage no more than 225mm/9in high. Its colour is a reddish green overlaid with a silver sheen. It would look good in tubs in a town garden, contrasted perhaps with the cabbagy fat shapes of aeoniums or houseleeks. Bronze cordyline is another Overbecks plant that would thrive in the sheltered microclimate of a courtyard, its strappy leaves paired with mounds of soft silver *Convolvulus cneorum*.

If you have not the heart to risk murdering phormiums, then you must turn to less dramatic substitutes: the fine tall leaves of crocosmia, stiff fans of iris foliage, or *Gladiolus byzantinus* are all easier to grow. The bronze-leaved *Crocosmia* 'Solfaterre' is probably the closest you will get to the bronze phormium effect, dramatic with orange gazanias. A green-leaved crocosmia, perhaps the startlingly red-flowered 'Lucifer', can be paired with a bronze-leaved dahlia and yellow coreopsis for a fiery late-summer show. The crocosmia's leaves have a pleasing pleated texture, with deeply incised veins running from leaf tip to base. They emerge in March and are still enthusiastically green and bright in October.

## A BLEND OF HERBS

A small formal herb garden is an ideal place to play the foliage-contrast game. All herbs are by definition foliage plants, and within this one small subsection there is an infinite variety of form: angelica, fennel, and the tightly

*Iris pseudacorus 'Variegata' seen here in June with yellow flowers scattered amongst the handsome striped leaves. This needs moist conditions to grow well.*

curled mossy effect of parsley, greatly underestimated as a foliage plant. Few other plants have such emerald intensity and the crimped, curled, complicated leaves have no substitute. Contrast it with handsomely dissected lovage, fat juicy spikes of chive, round leaves of basil, narrow olive-coloured foliage of rosemary and the small, glaucous spoon-shaped leaves of rue. Colour and texture also have an important part to play in arranging the most effective juxtapositions of herbs, but form comes first.

In the enchanting walled garden at FELBRIGG, where at any moment you expect to see the original owner, William Windham, in late-seventeenth-century frock coat, bending to pick pinks and tansy, there is a fine, informal collection of herbs in the border by the dovecot. Golden-variegated sage grows in front of motherwort, golden thyme in front of angelica, woodruff with plain sage, woad (*Isatis tinctoria*) behind golden feverfew, tansy with fennel. In the symmetrical herb garden at HARDWICK HALL, fennel together with golden hops grown up poles provide regular vertical accents throughout the whole of the scheme. Bay will do the same job, but with more *gravitas*. Fennel is a plant that is equally good in close-up or in long-shot. Examined closely, the foliage is gorgeous – fine, thin, filmy, beautifully arranged. Seen from a distance, the plant is equally striking. It makes a bold vertical. The parts may be diaphanous, but the whole is unequivocally well-defined. Fennel is also used in the mixed borders at Felbrigg and makes a fine dramatic group with *Crambe cordifolia* and the grey-leaved *Romneya coulteri*. This is bronze fennel rather than green, however both are equally easy to grow. Having such fine thread-like foliage, it is an ideal companion for a plant such as crambe, which has huge coarse leaves very much like a hogweed's; another cabbage leaf together with this would make an indigestible mix. Likewise, the airiness of the fennel would be uselessly dissipated if it was combined with an equally feathery plant such as dill. Aralia would be a good companion for fennel. So would *Sedum spectabile* or the purple-leaved *S. telephium maximum* 'Atropurpureum'.

## THE MERITS OF MAHONIA

Mahonia has the same gift as fennel. It is pleasing whatever view you take of it, and has the added advantage of being evergreen: fennel dives underground in winter. Mahonias are also superb in shade and, with a little judicious cutting back from time to time (best done after the shrub has flowered), keep a handsome if slightly gaunt outline with minimum assistance. The foliage is pinnate, which is to say that each leaf is made up of a series of leaflets arranged in matching pairs along the leaf's rib, with a terminal flourish of a leaflet at the very end. This is an agreeable form of foliage. Ash trees have it. So do the aralia and the mimosa. Mahonia leaves are normally dark glossy green, but some varieties, such as *M. aquifolium* 'Atropurpurea' and *M. × wagneri* 'Undulata', take on a bronze-purple finish in winter. The finest of the tribe, *M. lomariifolia*, is not reliably hardy, but will thrive in sheltered town gardens and in the generally

*Being evergreen, the mahonias are a particularly useful tribe and all have striking pinnate leaves composed of pairs of toothed leaflets. They thrive in shade.*

balmy quarter of south-west England. It has magnificently pinnate leaves, often as many as twenty pairs of leaflets arranged along the rib. There are upright spikes of flowers at the beginning of the year, but they are not scented. If you want scent, or worry about your plants catching a chill, choose *M. lomariifolia*'s daughter *M.* × 'Charity' instead.

One mahonia at least is an indispensable attribute in a garden. You could underplant it with shiny *Epimedium* × *rubrum* as they do at ASCOTT. At OVERBECKS Mr Tony Murdoch uses the tender *M. acanthifolia* against the rock wall of a big west-facing border. Its companions are a spiky purple phormium and a big group of the shuttlecock fern (*Matteuccia struthiopteris*). At TRERICE, mahonias are used in the striking yellow and purple borders in the courtyard in front of the house. *Mahonia lomariifolia* accompanies a neat-leaved purple berberis, used with the lance leaves of tradescantia and sisyrinchium. *Mahonia* × 'Charity' contrasts with the small crinkled leaves of a purple pittosporum and a neat mound of *Coronilla glauca*.

## CRAMBES AND RODGERSIAS

*Crambe cordifolia* needs space in a garden. It has huge hogweed leaves topped with panicles of tiny white flowers, which hover as delicately over the coarse foliage as fireflies over a hippopotamus. Its cousin, *Crambe maritima* (sea kale), which still grows wild on the shingle beaches of the south and east coasts of Britain, has smaller, wavy leaves, very much like a cabbage's, but with an attractive glaucous sheen. It is a handsome foliage plant and – the acid test – does not need to parade its flowers to guarantee entry into a planting scheme. Gertrude Jekyll was very fond of it and used it in her grand flower-border at Munstead. 'The front of the border has some important foliage giving a distinct blue effect; prominent among it sea kale. The flower stems are cut hard back in the earlier summer, and it is now in handsome fresh leaf.' She used it at either end of her border, with yucca, blue lyme grass and lamb's ear. At BENINGBROUGH it is also used in a grey scheme close to the house, its large, crinkled leaves

Rodgersia sambucifolia, *seen here with summer flowers, is slow to establish but has excellent foliage like that of a horse chestnut, each leaflet deeply ribbed.*

contrasting with the finer foliage of artemisia, flax, achillea and anthemis.

Rodgersia is a supremely handsome foliage plant, but most varieties need damp soil to flourish. *Rodgersia podophylla* will survive an occasional drought. It has palmate leaves, each of the five large leaflets radiating like the fingers of a hand. When it first emerges, it is a rich bronze-brown but fades to green as the season advances. At POWIS it is beautifully situated under a low spreading bush of a Japanese maple, *Acer palmatum* 'Dissectum Atropurpureum' – not the ideal spot for a plant that likes moist soil, you would have thought, but here it is certainly happy enough. At THE COURTS a great clump of it spreads over the banks of the lake, first bronze, then green, then broken up by the sprays of pink-buff flowers which start thrusting through in June. At DUNHAM MASSEY rodgersia is also by the water's edge, not *R.* *podophylla* but *R. tabularis* (now to be known as *Astilboides t.*) round simple leaves draped over a central stalk, each one a perfect Peter Rabbit umbrella. The edges of each leaf are slightly scalloped and grow about 900mm/3ft high. Not many leaves are held in this endearing way and though not as immediately arresting as the jagged leaves of the horse-chestnut-like *R. podophylla*, it makes a pleasant patch beside the stream, with the deeply cut foliage of *Actaea rubra*, spiky leaves of *Iris laevigata*, wands of willow gentian and fat clumps of bergenia.

## CATALOGUE OF PLANTS

### Acanthus (Bear's breeches)
*Deciduous perennial   Height and spread 1.2 × 1.2m/4 × 4ft*
Though generally deciduous, in a mild winter acanthus will not die back completely. If it does disappear, it can be slow to get going again in spring. It is a supreme foliage plant. *A. spinosus* has leaves at least 600mm/2ft long, each one deeply lobed and cut, in dark, glossy green. *A. mollis* has softer, cabbagy leaves, broader and less deeply cut than its cousin's. Both have spikes of hooded flowers, which last well into late autumn. On its own it combines well with stonework and statuary and becomes itself an architectural extravaganza. In a mixed planting it needs plenty of space round it, for the leaves mound up to make an all-smothering cover. At ICKWORTH it gives weight and importance to a planting of variegated philadelphus.

### Acer (Maple)
*Deciduous shrub or tree   Height and spread varies widely*
Excellent with ferns and azaleas, the maples seem to consort most naturally with plants of acid soils. Most of the tribe have lobed leaves, some deeply dissected. 'Laciniatum' and 'Dissectum' are the names to look for if you want a very lacy variety.

The Japanese maples typically make low spreading bushes, rather slow-growing, with leaves that colour all shades of orange and red in the autumn. They are used to great effect in the fern garden at SIZERGH, where after sixty years they have made impressive spreading shapes. *Acer palmatum dissectum* is used here with the soft hairy foliage of *Salix lanata*. Rodgersia grows under the spreading branches of *Acer palmatum atropurpureum*.

*The fiery autumn foliage of a Japanese maple planted against the south front at Hinton Ampner.* **Magnolia grandiflora** *provides a sober backdrop.*

### Angelica archangelica
*Deciduous biennial   Height and spread 1.8m × 900mm/6 × 3ft*
Only the the most besotted gardener would want a whole border of this, as Margery Fish did at East Lambrook Manor, but, liberated from the herb patch, angelica makes a startling contribution to mixed planting schemes. It looks particularly good against a plain dark background such as a yew hedge, where the fine, statuesque shape of the whole plant can be displayed in clean relief. The leaves are large, divided and in early spring a brilliant lush green. The plant is usually biennial: the first year it concentrates on leaf production and in the second it throws up a great stem topped with round umbels of creamy-green flowers. It grows anywhere, even in deep shade, provided this is moist and rich. It is a liberal self-seeder and a bully with respect to delicate neighbours. If you want to dictate terms, cut off the flower-heads before the seed starts to drop.

### Choisya ternata (Mexican orange blossom)

*Evergreen shrub   Height and spread 1.8 ×
1.5m/6 × 5ft*

This would be a winner even without its scented
white flowers, borne in late spring. It is a peerless
shrub, entirely without vices. It will grow in full
sun or deep shade, does well on all types of soil
and needs no fussing. In a hard winter, foliage
may get cut back or spoiled by freezing winds,
but it is the work of a moment to chop this out in
late spring. In very exposed gardens a sheltered
position will help it develop its full potential. The
glossy evergreen leaves are trifoliate (three
leaflets in a triangular pattern, joined at the base)
and make a superb background for later-
flowering lilies or Japanese anemones.

*The cardoon,* **Cynara cardunculus** *is a close relative of the
edible artichoke. It has less succulent flower heads,
though finer foliage with leaves sometimes 1.5m/5ft long.*

### Cynara (Cardoon)

*Deciduous perennial   Height and spread 1.8 ×
1.2m/6 × 4ft*

*C. cardunculus* is a rather more decorative version
of the edible artichoke, *C. scolymus*. It has longer,
more deeply cut leaves and, usually, more flower-
heads on each great branching stem. Its all-or-
nothing characteristics (a huge smothering
mound of foliage when it is above ground, a
gaping hole when it is not) make it quite a tricky
plant to place well. The foliage is at its shining,
silvery best in the first half of summer and, unlike
most of the silvers, this relishes damp, rich soil. A
very tough winter may kill it off, but clumps are
generally hardy once they are well established.
Spring is the best time to settle them in. The
edible artichoke makes a splendidly decorative
feature in a formal vegetable garden. They stand
like sentinels in the vegetable garden at
TINTINHULL, underplanted with old-fashioned
purple granny's bonnets.

### Euphorbia (Spurge)

*Evergreen or deciduous shrubs and
perennials   Height and spread varies widely*

This invaluable family embraces a vast array of
types: glaucous trailers, such as *E. myrsinites*, with
waxy blue leaves, each ending in a vivid lime
green head of flowers, and huge sculptural
uprights like the many forms of *E. characias* and
*E. characias wulfenii*, with oblong leaves arranged
around dramatic 1.2m/4ft stems. From March
onwards these are topped with the sulphurous-
looking flower-heads that are the spurges'
speciality. At COTEHELE a fine plant of *E. characias*
sits under the shelter of a wall, together with a
pink climbing rose and a shrubby bush of *Phlomis
fruticosa*. At KNIGHTSHAYES forms of the same
euphorbia are used in an island bed planted up in
the shelter of light woodland.

### Fatsia japonica

*Evergreen shrub   Height and spread 2.4 × 2.4m/
8 × 8ft*

*Fatsia japonica* is understated, elegant, a
designer's dream. It has huge evergreen leaves,
nine lobed fingers joining to make a stiff,
spreading hand, each leaf held on a strong stalk,
more than 300mm/1ft long. It likes shade, which
makes it ideal for dressing up gloomy sub-
basement gardens, and though it looks tropically
exotic, is perfectly hardy. The leaves are
exceptionally glossy and seem to bring light into
corners where there is none. Like ivy, it flowers in
winter, with large clusters of creamy balls. If they
are pollinated properly (flies do the job) they set
into black berries. If a plant starts to overreach
itself, branches can be cut out at ground level, but
it needs no regular pruning.

### Helleborus

*Evergreen perennial   Height and spread 600 ×
600mm/2 × 2ft*

*H. argutifolius* (*syn. H corsicus*) has perhaps the
most handsome leaf of this extravagantly well-
endowed family. The leaves are three-lobed, each
of the stiff leaflets joined to the top of the stalk
and edged all round with mock prickles. The
green is matt and olive, a perfect foil for the great
mounds of cup-shaped flowers that open in
midwinter. It grows equally happily in full sun or
shade and looks excellent with pulmonarias or
undercarpeted with the silver-smudged leaves of
*Cyclamen coum*. The later-flowering Lenten
hellebore, *H. orientalis*, has more leaflets to each
leaf, smooth, not prickled, held in glossy fans.
Good forms of *H. × sternii*, such as 'Blackthorn
Strain', silver foliage flushed with pink and pink
flowers are also worth seeking. *H. multifidus* is
another striking hellebore with leaves composed
of many narrow leaflets. Old leaves should be cut
away before the flowers start coming through in
late winter. This helps to prevent the spread of
botrytis, this plant's only enemy.

*Mounds of acanthus frame a doorway at Beningbrough with* **Vitis vinifera** *clothing the wall behind. This is an easier vine to place than large-leaved* **Vitis coignetiae.**

*A bold group of* **Yucca recurvifolia** *casting bold shadows on the grass in the column garden at Montacute. These dramatic plants are best seen in isolation.*

### Vitis (vine)

*Deciduous climber    Height and spread 6 × 6m/20 × 20ft*

Unfortunately, the most spectacular vines are not those with the best grapes. As with the cardoon, a difficult choice must be made between pleasing eye and pleasing stomach. The grand-daddy of the tribe is *V. coignetiae* with enormous heart-shaped, floppy leaves, rough-textured as a terrier's coat and, on satisfactory soil, colouring brilliantly in autumn. It is built on Tarzan lines, however, and should not be used in a small garden. *V. vinifera* 'Purpurea' is more manageable; leaves are smaller and the growth, supported by curling tendrils, is not so vigorous. It grows over the arbour at MOSELEY OLD HALL, together with *Clematis flammula*, and backs one of the long borders at BENINGBROUGH with honeysuckle, clematis and old pink roses. *Vitis belaii*, found in several National Trust gardens, looks like a fairly ordinary vine until the autumn when its leaves turn a dazzling scarlet. It is one of

the stars of the vine collection at Kew, but its origin is obscure.

### Yucca

*Evergreen shrub    Height and spread 1.2 × 1.2m/4 × 4ft*

Think of the desert before you plant yucca, for this is where it comes from and this is what it needs: full sun and a fast-draining, light soil. These are statuesque, somewhat stagy plants, happier hobnobbing with urns and statues than with dumpy English perennials. *Y. gloriosa* has

rapier-sharp points to its long sword leaves; *Y. filamentosa* is kinder, with leaves up to 450mm/ 18in long, of a soft, glaucous green. Plants of this variety mark the corners of the beds in the formal Norah Lindsay parterre at BLICKLING with pools of anthemis, helenium and leucanthemum round their feet. The stiffer *Y. gloriosa* is similarly used in the fan-shaped parterre at GAWTHORPE HALL. Each bed is edged with dwarf purple berberis and filled with golden privet. The yuccas mark the base of each fan spoke.

# TEXTURE

The texture of a plant's leaves is a less eye-catching attribute than its colour and shape, one of those quiet pleasures that you take for granted, like the softness of wool or the shininess of a well-polished table. But leaves, too, can be woolly or smooth, shiny or matt, prickly or silky soft, crinkled or plain, waxy, sticky or slippery as an ice cube. Although we may not perceive texture as immediately as other specific qualities, it is an important part of a plant's personality. John Gerard, the famous Elizabethan horticulturist, certainly recognized this and his *Herball* (1597) is full of references to the tactile qualities of the plants he described. 'The great Mouse-eare hath great and large leaves, thick and full of substance: the stalkes and leaves bee hoary and white, with a silken mossinesse in handling like silke, pleasant and faire in view.'

## LEAF SURFACE

The massive variation in the texture of plants is not an act put on for our tactile delight but is usually their response to a particular set of growing conditions or problems. The hairs on the leaves of an edelweiss that give it its distinctive, woolly appearance protect it from the intense light of high altitudes. Hairs also act like a fur coat to insulate a plant from the worst extremes of temperature. Some of the woolliest plants in existence grow where the climate is most extreme, in deserts or freezing upland steppes. A hairy covering also reduces the amount of water that is lost through the leaves by transpiration. The familiar lamb's ear, *Stachys lanata* is unlikely to die of drought in a British garden, but its leaves developed their dense covering of silky hair to cope with the far less propitious conditions of its native habitat in the Caucasus and Iran. In a laboratory experiment, scientists compared the transpiration rate of ordinary lamb's ear leaves with ones that had been carefully shaved of their hair. The shorn leaves lost moisture at twice the rate of the ordinary ones.

Often a plant's specific epithet will give you an indication of its texture. The *lanata* of *Stachys lanata* means woolly. *Tomentosa*, as in *Achillea tomentosa*, also translates as something that is soft and furry to the touch. The leaves of lamb's ear, some verbascums and salvias, such as *Salvia argentea*, and the willow, *Salix lanata*, are so densely hairy that they not only feel furry but also appear as silver rather than green.

*Contrasts of shape and texture at Tintinhull with prostrate juniper, shiny bergenia and fountains of hemerocallis in the pool garden (above). The soft matt texture of moss throws into relief the polished fronds of hart's tongue fern (opposite).*

*The bull bay,* Magnolia grandiflora, *is a handsome evergreen shrub or tree with leaves as shiny as gloss paint.*

Other leaves which do not need this kind of protection from the extremes of climate use hairs for different purposes. The hairs that make both hop and bramble leaves rough to the touch are not dense enough to change the leaf colour, but are slightly hooked so that along with tendrils and thorns, they help the plant scramble through neighbours towards the light. Hairy leaves also seem less palatable to slugs and snails than smooth ones, so may have been developed by some low-growing plants as a protection against predators.

Prickles provide an even better defence. The spines on leaves are often an extension of leaf veins, hardened and sharpened to become an effective weapon against browsers and gatherers. Holly is one of the most familiar of this group, but thistles and the leaves of the sea holly (*Eryngium maritimum*) have also gone through the same process of adaptation. This gives them a strong outline as well as a particular sort of texture – certainly not friendly, but memorable. Members of the cactus family have taken the process to extremes and got rid of their leaves altogether, leaving only vicious spines in their place.

The highly polished leaves of plants such as holly, choisya, *Magnolia grandiflora*, camellia, aucuba, escallonia, and fatsia are useful in planting schemes because they are evergreen. But their glossy texture adds to their interest. The shiny leaf surfaces reflect the light, which seems to make the foliage a particularly intense green. Their shininess provides a superb foil for grey plants such as senecio and artemisia, which are naturally matt in texture.

The most pleasing plant associations therefore will take into account the texture of foliage as well as a plant's form, colour and habit of growth. This may seem like juggling with too many balls in the air, but it is not difficult to move plants about if they are still in pots. The best thing is to play about with groups of pots, shifting plants into different positions and walking round to look at them from every possible angle before you finally anchor them into the soil. There is rarely one perfect answer.

## CONTRASTING TEXTURES AT POWIS

In the incomparable garden at POWIS CASTLE the south-east facing borders planted up on the terraces hacked out centuries ago from the red sandstone are an object lesson in the use of contrasting textures. On the aviary terrace, the matt, felted, crinkled leaves of *Phlomis chrysophylla* set off the simple, dark, glossy leaves of the *Hebe* 'Amy'. The great cabbagy, woolly leaves of *Salvia argentea* are used with the springy, heather-like foliage of *Fabiana imbricata violacea*. *Rosa glauca* (syn. *R. rubrifolia*) with glaucous, steel-blue leaves is underplanted with a low-growing spurge, *Euphorbia seguieriana niciciana*, blue-grey also, but with a rich, waxy bloom on its leaves, quite different from the dry, cool, dull texture of the rose. This small euphorbia is an outstanding plant, with trailing stems of feathery foliage arranged in whorls round the stem. Its cousin *E. myrsinites*, with rather bolder, but equally waxy-looking leaves, is also a good front-of-the-border star. Cineraria (*Senecio bicolor cineraria*), its stems and leaves done over with a flour dredger, adds another completely different texture to this group.

The supreme foliage plant, melianthus, with handsome pinnate leaves about 300mm/1ft long, has the best glaucous foliage of all. It is not reliably hardy, but you can take cuttings in autumn and overwinter them away from frost. At Powis its steely blue-green leaves contrast with the glossy foliage of the purple *Hebe* 'La Seduisante'. On the top terrace it is combined with fatshedera which has huge hand-shaped glossy leaves like a fig's. In the same border, the handsome glaucous tobacco plant, *Nicotiana glauca*, is used with the shiny leaves of the blood flower, *Asclepias curassavica*, a sticky pool of *Mimulus glutinosus* lying along the front. This is gardening of a very high order indeed, but there is no reason why lesser mortals should not aspire to similar effects, given similar advantages of aspect and site.

Some excellent plants are difficult to place because they change their habits so radically during their lifespan. *Meconopsis regia* is a case in point. This is a relative of the well-known blue Himalayan poppy, though little about it

Phlomis fruticosa (*Jerusalem sage*) is a spreading, evergreen shrub with thickly felted grey-green foliage akin to that of sage.

## POWIS CASTLE
### Top Terrace border

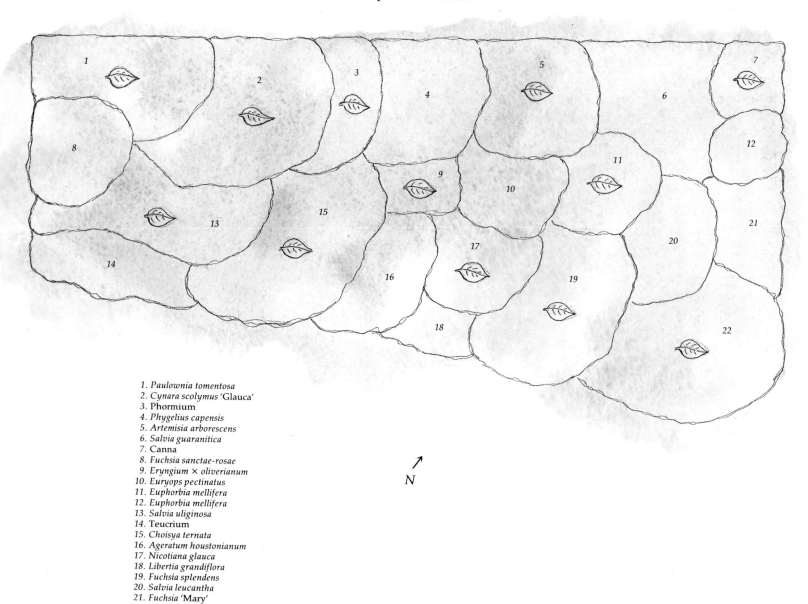

1. *Paulownia tomentosa*
2. *Cynara scolymus* 'Glauca'
3. Phormium
4. *Phygelius capensis*
5. *Artemisia arborescens*
6. *Salvia guaranitica*
7. Canna
8. *Fuchsia sanctae-rosae*
9. *Eryngium × oliverianum*
10. *Euryops pectinatus*
11. *Euphorbia mellifera*
12. *Euphorbia mellifera*
13. *Salvia uliginosa*
14. Teucrium
15. *Choisya ternata*
16. *Ageratum houstonianum*
17. *Nicotiana glauca*
18. *Libertia grandiflora*
19. *Fuchsia splendens*
20. *Salvia leucantha*
21. *Fuchsia* 'Mary'
22. *Argyranthemum maderense*

N

DIMENSIONS: 6.4m×11m (21ft×36ft)

would lead you to suspect the connection. For the first part of its life (it is monocarpic and dies after flowering), it sits close to the ground, making a handsome rosette of large, extremely hairy leaves, the edges toothed like the leaves of an oriental poppy. It holds raindrops in the same dazzling way as alchemilla, turning each one into a perfect round bead. The leaves are a most unusual colour, unlike anything else you are likely to find – pale green, overlaid with a hint of buff, which is perhaps the effect of its furry coat. As it is so very flat, you give it a position at the front of a planting, where you can regularly admire the superb texture of its leaves. For the first year, or perhaps two, you are proud and gratified at the amount of attention it is given by visitors and nominate it for a prominent place in the foliage plants' Hall of Fame.

In the second part of its life, however, it astounds you by throwing up a thick flowering stem which grows as fast as a pantomime beanstalk. The supply of leaves, constantly renewed during the first year with fresh young growth from the centre of the rosette, suddenly dries up and all available effort is put into a mammoth display of papery yellow poppy flowers which open in succession on the sturdy 1.2m/4ft stem between June and July. Although it can be tricky to accommodate such a Jekyll and Hyde character, nevertheless the texture of the young leaves of *Meconopsis regia*, more like animal fur than vegetable tissue, makes it an invaluable foliage plant.

*Though magnolias are chiefly thought of as flowering trees, many varieties have foliage good enough to sustain interest through the rest of the growing season.*

## WATERSIDE PLANTING AT DUNHAM MASSEY

The various textures of leaves most closely resemble different fabrics: silk, satin, linen, angora, tweed, corduroy, woollens. *Veratrum nigrum* is like the permanently pleated silk of a Fortuny dress. Its leaves are not the slightest bit hairy. Texture is created by the way that each leaf is deeply creased into a series of folds or furrows that stretch from the leaf's base to its tip. The midrib is quite stiff, and as the leaves unfurl they make handsome, overlapping curves of green. The rhizomes do best in moist, light soil in a place where they will be partially shaded. A thick mulch of compost or peat in May will help to create the kind of conditions they enjoy. Unfortunately, slugs love them. Like hostas, they must be well protected against attack. The leaves grow no taller than those of hostas, but in August the veratrum sends up a tall spike packed with black-red flowers. It is well used in a streamside planting at DUNHAM MASSEY. In front of it are mounds of downy-haired alchemilla; behind, large clumps of *Ligularia dentata* 'Desdemona', which has heart-shaped leaves of a shiny, metallic green, backed with mahogany. The form of the three leaves differs markedly, which is of course an important factor in the success of the combination, but this success is enhanced by the corresponding contrasts in texture: pleated silk veratrum, alchemilla with the texture of Viyella shirts and dull satin ligularia.

The whole of this particular bog garden is rich in good foliage plants, which luxuriate in the rich, damp conditions. At the eastern end of the border is a stand of white Rugosa roses. Here again the specific epithet *rugosa* tells you what to expect by way of texture. It comes from the Latin word meaning wrinkled or creased. All Rugosa leaves are rigidly corrugated, pleasantly rough to the touch and a particularly fresh and vivid green. There is also a practical advantage to this texture. It protects the leaves against black spot, for the spores do not easily find a foothold on these wrinkled surfaces. The crinkling gives the leaves a matt effect which contrasts well with the foliage of the low-growing *Berberis candidula* alongside. The leaves of the berberis are thin, narrow and highly polished on the upper surface, the undersides a powdery silver. A further contrast in leaf texture is offered by the clumps of *Hosta sieboldiana* 'Elegans' which adjoin both berberis and rose. The hosta's leaves have a glaucous, waxy finish, almost luminous in effect. Here again, contrasts of texture added to variety of leaf shape make a most satisfying plant group.

## COMPOSING WITH CONTRASTS

It would be silly to get too precious about this business. Gardening is for fun, not for agony. If you can hold in your head just a handful of different kinds of leaf texture, plants can slot roughly into one or other type. Then you choose plants from differing batches, rather than a group in which the leaves are essentially similar. Plain green hollies and camellias have much the same properties; so do pulmonarias and comfrey, which are both rough-textured and hairy. Many grey-leaved plants have rather a dull matt texture, but there are notable exceptions such as *Convolvulus cneorum* which has narrow leaves, magnificently burnished and shining. Sedums, some sempervivums and the rosettes of London pride (*Saxifraga* × *urbium*) all share a similar fleshy, smooth, stiff texture. The leaves of *Verbascum dumulosum* have the same mealy, floury quality as those of *Senecio* 'White Diamond'. Some plants, such as philadelphus, prunus and honeysuckle, are neutral in this respect. Variegated plants rarely have well-textured leaves: the bi-colouring is enough of a *divertissement*. Leaving out the plants with coloured leaves, purple and gold as well as variegated, most other good foliage plants will have a strong tactile quality. It is impossible to pass a bush of *Phlomis italica* without reaching out to touch its soft, hairy leaves and rub them gently between the fingers. Like the rest of this family, it likes dry, well-drained soil in full sun, where it will quickly grow into a reasonably upright shrub, about 900mm/ 3ft high. Both the leaves and the stems are richly furred, and it has terminal spikes of pink-mauve lipped flowers in midsummer.

## DUNHAM MASSEY
### Bog garden

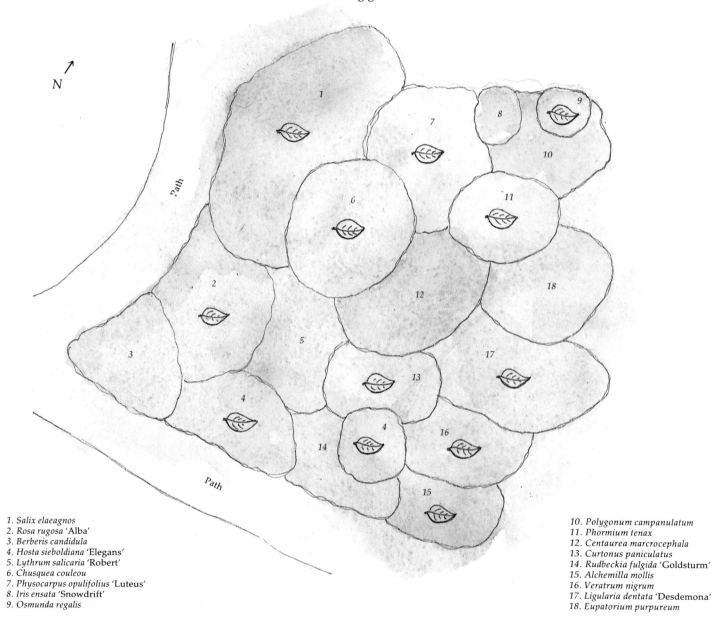

1. *Salix elaeagnos*
2. *Rosa rugosa* 'Alba'
3. *Berberis candidula*
4. *Hosta sieboldiana* 'Elegans'
5. *Lythrum salicaria* 'Robert'
6. *Chusquea couleou*
7. *Physocarpus opulifolius* 'Luteus'
8. *Iris ensata* 'Snowdrift'
9. *Osmunda regalis*

10. *Polygonum campanulatum*
11. *Phormium tenax*
12. *Centaurea marcrocephala*
13. *Curtonus paniculatus*
14. *Rudbeckia fulgida* 'Goldsturm'
15. *Alchemilla mollis*
16. *Veratrum nigrum*
17. *Ligularia dentata* 'Desdemona'
18. *Eupatorium purpureum*

DIMENSIONS: *17.3m×17.3m (58ft×58ft)*

*The low spreading Sedum × 'Ruby Glow' has neat waxy grey-blue foliage overlaid in July
and August with wide heads of rose-coloured flowers. This is an invaluable front of the border
plant, to contrast perhaps with the matt texture of a mossy green saxifrage.*

The dramatic *Viburnum rhytidophyllum* is another shrub that demands to be touched. It has large, elliptical leaves up to 200mm/8in long, as deeply wrinkled as an elephant's knee. The texture is like sandpaper and the underside of each leaf is covered with fine hair which turns the green to grey. It makes a strong-growing evergreen screen, up to 3.6m/12ft high, the bold leaves hanging like tournament favours. At WALLINGTON it is grouped with philadelphus and a dark cut-leaved elder, *Sambucus nigra* 'Laciniata'. Its flowers are not a great asset, heavy-handed clumps of extremely off-white, but the red and black berries that replace them are worth having. It is not suitable for heavy shade: something odd happens to the leaves in this situation and they are smitten with a bad case of the droops.

## TEXTURE IN LONG-SHOT

Specific textures are also created by the effect of leaves *en masse*. Taken individually, leaflets of yew are no great shakes, but a treeful of them is quite a different proposition. A handsome matt green hedge of yew provides an incomparable background to herbaceous plantings, or contrasts with the paler, glossier green of grass to make more restrained garden vistas. The hedge itself will have different characteristics of texture depending on whether it is closely clipped and angular or softened by a designer stubble of fresh new growth. Those in a hurry use Leyland cypress instead of yew, but the texture is not so close and the structure not so solid as a bastion of our own native evergreen. Since individual leaves and leaflets are often so tiny, sometimes reduced to needles, the texture of many of the conifers depends on the whole rather than on the parts. Junipers, swamp cypresses, cryptomeria, picea, and abies all work on the same principle of mass effect. Some are more accommodating than others. Swamp cypress (*Taxodium distichum*) is only for the largest gardens. Juniper is endlessly versatile and can provide a low, spreading mattress of glaucous blue, *J. horizontalis*, or in the variety 'Skyrocket', a tall column 1.8m/6ft high, though less than 300mm/1ft wide.

*Cypress foliage* en masse, *here at Killerton has a different texture to that of an individual leaflet examined at close range.*

## CATALOGUE OF PLANTS

### Cytisus battandieri (Moroccan broom)
*Deciduous shrub    Height and spread 4.5 × 3m/
15 × 10ft*
Wise gardeners will give this lax-growing shrub
the protection of a wall, for it is not fully hardy,
particularly in northern gardens. The silvery
leaves are silky soft and have a gorgeous sheen.
The stumpy racemes of bright yellow flowers
smell strongly of pineapple and cover the
branches in May and June. It needs no regular
pruning, but unwanted growths can be cut back
after flowering. It grows luxuriantly on the south-
facing wall behind the herbaceous border at
BODNANT, together with *Hydrangea sargentiana*
and *Actinidia kolomikta*. Spiky leaves of *Phormium
tenax* provide an excellent contrast in the
foreground. At TATTON PARK it grows with
eucryphia, olearia and *Itea ilicifolia* in the
buttressed enclosures of the big L-shaped border
to the west of the house.

### Hydrangea sargentiana
*Deciduous shrub    Height and spread 1.8 × 1.8m/
6 × 6ft*
This handsome hydrangea needs moist, rich soil
and medium shade to give of its best. The leaves
are large, up to 250mm/10in long, and have a
distinctive rough texture like sharkskin, which
contrasts well with the small, glossy leaves of a
shrub such as berberis. Lacy mauve heads of
flowers appear in midsummer. It does not need
regular pruning, but any shoots damaged in
winter should be cut out in early spring. A mulch
of manure or compost in April will help to keep
the roots cool and well fed. A fine specimen of *H.
sargentiana* stands in the shrubbery at PECKOVER,
where its companions are a ginkgo and a
beautiful *Sophora japonica*. It also grows well in
the walled garden at NYMANS, together with
nothofagus, stewartia, hoheria and Winter's bark
(*Drimys winteri*).

### Juniperus (Juniper)
*Evergreen shrub or tree    Height and spread varies
widely with species*
Juniper is one of the many conifers that depend
for their effect on a mass of foliage. Habits differ
widely, but all the 'blue' junipers have the same
matt, densely feathery, glaucous texture. *J.
horizontalis* 'Glauca' is completely prostrate and
very slow-growing. It will take at least ten years to
cover 1.5m/5ft. Cyclamen are lovely with it,
particularly the marbled foliage of *C. hederifolium*.
*Juniperus scopulorum* 'Sky Rocket' does the
opposite thing, zooming straight up rather than
out, eventually making a thin column 1.8m/6ft
high, but no more than 300mm/1ft across. At
KNIGHTSHAYES a specimen of *Juniperus recurva
coxii*, named after Farrer's travelling companion
E.H.M. Cox, is skirted round with the silver-blue
foliage of *Picea pungens* 'Glauca Globosa'.
Junipers also feature in the exuberant tree
plantings at ASCOTT.

### Lysichiton americanus (Skunk cabbage, bog arum)
*Deciduous perennial    Height and spread 900 ×
900mm/3 × 3ft*
Rich bog is the right home for this unusual plant,
a cousin of our wild arum. It has showier spathes
than the British native and is bigger in all its
parts. After the yellow spathes come sheaves of
enormous glossy leaves, waist high when the
plant has settled and is growing strongly. They
have thick midribs and should be admired from
afar as they smell worse than a cesspit if you
touch them. At SIZERGH it grows by the rock pools
together with groups of *Primula florindae*. At
TRENGWAINTON, where a stream borders
woodland, it grows with rodgersias, the round fat
leaves of peltiphyllum and a clump of the
cultivated arum, *Zantedeschia aethiopica* 'Green
Jade'. The lacy texture of ferns such as *Osmunda*

*regalis* also provides an excellent contrast to these
highly polished leaves. *L. camtschatcensis* is
similar but slightly smaller with white spathes.

*Skunk cabbage,* Lysichiton americanus, *in the stream
garden at Trengwainton.*

### Salix lanata (Woolly willow)
*Deciduous shrub    Height and spread 900 × 900mm/
3 × 3ft*
This slow-growing willow is ideal for damp,
waterside locations. It has rounded, down-
covered leaves of an outstanding soft texture.
Small greyish-yellow catkins appear with the first
leaves in late spring and stand upright from the
twigs. It is used with the rosemary-leaved willow
(*Salix elaeagnos*) and the silver-leaved coyote
willow (*S. exigua*) in the willow garden at
KNIGHTSHAYES. It finds a natural home here, as it
does beside one of the rivulets in the rock garden
at SIZERGH. At HIDCOTE it is used on the rock bank
with other shrubs such as the glaucous Irish
juniper (*Juniperus communis* 'Hibernica'), the low-
growing *Cotoneaster adpressus*, various potentillas
and a dwarf Japanese pine (*Pinus densiflora*
'Umbraculifera').

### Salvia argentea

*Deciduous biennial/short-lived perennial   Height and spread 600 × 600mm/2 × 2ft*

Most of the salvias have undistinguished leaves and are grown for their fine hooded flowers, often of dazzling blue. This member of the sage family is a notable exception. It has large, silvery, thickly furred leaves, arranged in a flat, ground-hugging rosette. In a very well-drained sunny position, it is exceptionally eye-catching. If damp, it will rot. In July it throws up a stem of mauve-white flowers and seeds itself about quite easily. At TINTINHULL it has put itself alongside a stand of white sweet rocket and small clumps of the purple and yellow *Viola* 'Prince Henry'. The rounded, unfussy leaves of this salvia provide a useful contrast to the deeply cut ferny foliage of many other grey plants.

### Sedum (Ice plant)

*Deciduous perennial   Height and spread 600 × 450mm/24 × 18in*

The bigger sedums, varieties of *S. maximum*, *S. telephium*, and *S. spectabile*, all have juicy, succulent leaves, tempting enough to sink your teeth into, like some vegetarian vampire. The colour is a pale glaucous green, the texture waxy and slightly unreal. They are invaluable front-of-the-border plants and in late summer add to the mounds of solid foliage flat clusters of flowers in shades of pink and red. They are generously used at POWIS. On the apple slope terrace, *S. telephium* 'Ruprechtii', grey leaves tinged with pink, partners *Parahebe perfoliata* with stems of flowers piercing paired leaves. *Sedum* 'Ruby Glow' with purple-grey succulent foliage and *S. spectabile* stand behind the stiff skeletons of *Eryngium giganteum*. *Sedum* 'Autumn Joy', which Head Gardener Mr Jimmy Hancock splits and replants in March or early April, grows with mounds of *Geranium* 'Mavis Simpson'. Left to their own devices the big sedums splay out in an unattractive way as they grow taller, leaving a bald patch in the middle of the clump. Splitting and resetting the plants keeps clumps smaller and more compact.

### Stachys lanata (Lamb's ears)

*Semi-evergreen perennial   Height and spread 300 × 300mm/12 × 12in*

'Silver Carpet' is the non-flowering form of the well-known lamb's ears. Although it can look bedraggled in winter or after heavy summer rain, this is an invaluable low-growing plant, excellent with roses, as at BENINGBROUGH, where it makes a velvety carpet underneath bushes of the old pale pink rose 'Gruss an Aachen'. It prefers well-drained soil for, like most of the greys, it will rot away if it is too damp. It needs picking over regularly so that yellowing and withered leaves do not spoil the overall effect. It is a favourite plant for all white gardens, often used as an edging to borders or paths. You will find it in the white garden at BARRINGTON, its furry leaves well contrasted with the glaucous foliage of the pink 'Mrs Sinkins'.

### Verbascum (Mullein)

*Semi-evergreen biennial or perennial   Height and spread up to 1.8m × 900mm/6 × 3ft*

*V. dumulosum* is an alpine species with white, heavily felted leaves, matt rather than glossy like those of *Salvia argentea*, which sprout from a woody crown in spring. It has short spires, not more than 150mm/6in high, of large yellow flowers in midsummer. The tall herbaceous varieties have some of the best foliage of the tribe. *V. bombyciferum* is a biennial monster with enormous rough oval leaves, up to 900mm/3ft long, downy, matt and silver-white. It is a stately plant that does not need staking, but may be a martyr to the voracious caterpillars of the mullein moth which can strip a plant overnight. If you want to keep this verbascum as a foreground foliage feature, pinch out the flowering spike as soon as you see it forming. They look good with stands of the tall *Verbena bonariensis* behind.

*The clump forming perennial* **Rodgersia sambucifolia** *with heavily ribbed, corrugated leaves.*

# VARIEGATION

A variegated plant draws attention to itself as shamelessly as a starlet on her first publicity tour and therefore needs to be placed very carefully in the garden if it is not to overshadow other plants that may have just as much charm, though half the chutzpah. Because they always draw the eye, they need to be used sparingly. One variegated cornus, set perhaps against the dark background of a yew tree and partnered by the handsome glossy leaves of choisya, will shine out, each margined leaf clearly silhouetted against the plain backdrop. This is a soothing, comforting combination with plenty to feed the senses: the dense, matt black-green of the yew, where individual leaflets are so tiny that they merge into one light-absorbing mass; the light-reflecting leaves of the choisya, spread like hands in glossy mid-green; and the simple oval leaves of a cornus such as *C. alba* 'Elegantissima', pale grey-green with broad white margins.

If, however, there are other variegated plants nearby, they will lurk in the corner of the eye and, instead of standing peacefully in front of the cornus, quietly absorbing its pleasures, you will find that your attention is leaping from this to the next variegated clump, as restless as a migrating frog. The smaller the garden, the more restrained you will have to be in your use of variegated plants – which will be difficult, because among this group are to be found some of the most striking and irresistible foliage forms of all.

Some plants, of course, are less demanding than others; visually demanding, that is, rather than horticulturally. The

*The brilliantly variegated foliage of a tender abutilon thrown into sharp relief against a sober backdrop of plain green in the pool garden at Tintinhull.*

comfrey, *Symphytum × uplandicum* 'Variegatum', is extremely importunate, a great bully of a plant with leaves as coarse and as large as a dock's, but of a lovely grey-green colour, heavily margined with cream. When it is at its best, before and after the distraction of flowering in midsummer, it can knock out any spectator at a distance of ten paces. Aesthetic companions – elegant broom, astilbe, feathery achilleas – will be knocked out also. The comfrey needs something altogether tougher as its neighbour – angelica, perhaps, or the dark bulk of acanthus.

It follows, therefore, that if you are determined to have this variegated comfrey in a small patch, you will not be able to have much else that is variegated in close proximity. If, however, you choose more recessively variegated plants – the gently silvered leaves of *Cyclamen hederifolium*, the hairy cream-veined foliage of the tender creeping *Saxifraga stolonifera* or the grey-green *Fuchsia magellanica* 'Versicolor' which has leaves flushed and striped with pink and cream – you will be able to slide more variegated plants into a scheme. The choice is between one big shout, or a series of murmurs.

## FORMS OF VARIEGATION
Variegation itself takes many different forms, from such tricolor combinations as the white, pink and green of the climber *Actinidia kolomikta* and various bugles to the restrained marbling, cream on green, of the handsome winter foliage plant *Arum italicum marmoratum* (*A.i. pictum*). Startling white variegation, such as appears on some hostas, moves through various shades of cream to the cheerful yellow and green combinations of elaeagnus and holly. The

white tones will cool down a garden scheme; yellow will warm a dark and chilly corner. Elaeagnus, for instance, will lift sombre plantings of yew and ivy and a variety such as *E. pungens* 'Maculata' has the happy knack of flourishing in deep shade or full sun. It can become lax when growing in shade, and young plants, particularly, will benefit from having their new shoots cut back by half in spring to encourage a more bushy habit of growth. Variegation is often affected by the way we treat plants in the garden. An over-rich diet will persuade plants to become more green than cream. Sun and shade also have an effect on the final colour. In sun the variegated astrantia may change to green by early summer. In shade – and it will flourish in quite deep shade – the variegation remains most of the season.

Variegation is caused by lack of chlorophyll, an aberration which produces white and yellow stripes, spots and margins on variegated foliage. Where leaves are green-centred with a white margin, the green part (which is more vigorous) sometimes grows at a faster rate than the chlorophyll-starved band around the edge. This can result in leaves that look distorted and sick, as with the variegated solanum. Leaves that are splashed white in the centre – those of holly, elaeagnus, the variegated sycamore – do not have this problem, but are more likely to revert to plain green than the white-banded leaves.

In some variegated plants, the lack of chlorophyll in the leaves results in a distinct lack of vigour overall. The variegated shrub *Azara microphylla* 'Variegata', for instance, is often a poor thing, slow and much more susceptible to frost than its evergreen cousin. The elegant *Iris pallida* 'Variegata' with leaves striped in cream and grey clumps up far more slowly than the plain green form, and the variegated mock orange, *Philadelphus coronarius* 'Variegatus', is a reluctant guest, slow to grow and difficult to please, though *P.* 'Innocence Variegatus' is an excellent plant. Wherever possible, see a plant growing in ordinary garden conditions before you swoop in to buy. Some tricky plants in nurseries and garden centres are given the sort of protection and special care that may be impractical in the position that you have in mind for them.

Certain families of plants seem to favour certain patterns of variegation. Grasses and sedges, with the notable exception of the cross-banded *Miscanthus sinensis* 'Zebrinus', prefer their variegation in longitudinal stripes down the leaf. So do members of the Liliaceae: hemerocallis, lily of the valley, phormium and Solomon's seal.

Different forms of the same plant can be greatly dissimilar. *Brunnera macrophylla*, that invaluable filler-in with rough heart-shaped leaves and sprays of blue forget-me-not flowers, has two variegated forms. 'Hadspen Cream' has leaves edged in rich cream. Its markings are not so vivid as the form called 'Dawson's White', where the leaves are splashed with white and lots of it, but the former is the better garden plant. It makes a more sympathetic companion in most planting schemes than the vividly bi-coloured leaves of 'Dawson's White' and it does not scorch and brown as they do.

Though showy, variegated plants should not blind you to the fact that you still need to give thought to contrasts of form and texture within the plant group. The fine, delicate foliage of *Fuchsia magellanica* 'Versicolor' will contrast well with the fat juicy leaves and flat blocked flower-heads of *Sedum* 'Autumn Joy', but would be less effective teamed with deutzia or with a perennial such as Michaelmas daisy or solidago which has a similar simple leaf. Add yucca and ceratostigma to the fuchsia and sedum to make a bold late-summer group.

**SHRUBS FOR LARGE-SCALE PLANTING**

In large mixed borders, well-placed variegated shrubs can give order and balance to the planting scheme. In the big borders laid out by Graham Stuart Thomas at BENINGBROUGH, a white variegated dogwood is used with the golden-flowered Mount Etna broom, *Genista aetnensis*, anchored against the stately dark bulk of *Acanthus spinosus*. At WALLINGTON you will find the same dogwood, *Cornus alba*

*The unusual Himalayan lilac* Syringa emodii, *here at Overbecks in the variegated form*
*'Aureovariegata'. The flowers, borne in erect panicles in June are not so sweetly scented*
*as those of more common garden lilacs, but the leaves, up to 20cm/8in long, are remarkable.*

*Many forms of* Euonymus fortunei *are now available, with leaves variegated in silver or gold.*

'Elegantissima', in the border in front of the conservatory with lamb's ear (*Stachys lanata*) and a pale blue *Viola cornuta* sharing the ground in front of it. A 'Versicolor' fuchsia is fronted by a big group of agapanthus, whose bright, shiny strap leaves and blue globes of flowers look as well with this neighbour as with any you are likely to find after a year of searching. In the border against the house at LYTES CARY, the same pale dogwood is used with lavender and the tall leafy *Nicotiana sylvestris* to make a cool group of grey, white and green. Here, too, the popular *Euonymus fortunei* 'Emerald 'n' Gold' makes a vivid splash, planted with *Achillea* 'Moonshine' – feathery grey leaves and important flat flower-heads packed with yellow as bright as butter. In a mixed border at TRENGWAINTON, a large shrub of *Pittosporum crassifolium* 'Variegatum' with thick grey-green leathery leaves, margined in white, is underplanted with the handsome rosettes of *Eryngium alpinum* 'Amethyst'. Although this pittosporum grows like a native in west-coast gardens, as many Australasian species do, it is unlikely to survive winters farther north and east.

The Japanese angelica tree, *Aralia elata* 'Albo-variegata', has superb pinnate leaves up to 1.2m/4ft long. This plant is a star and needs a suitably important position in a garden, preferably in full sun. Although it grows fast when it is young, it slows down with age and rarely gets above 3.6m/12ft in height. At WALLINGTON, it stands alone as a specimen in the lawn. At DUNSTER it lords it over a planting of purple berberis and large purple-flowered hebes. At KNIGHTSHAYES it is soberly set off by an underplanting of handsome Lenten roses (*Helleborus orientalis*).

In larger shrub plantings, it may be appropriate for the choice of shrubs to be dictated by the style and period of the house they surround. Spotty laurel (*Aucuba japonica*), an archetypal Victorian favourite, is exactly what you expect to find in the wilderness walk at PECKOVER HOUSE, where there is a perfect period garden lying behind the handsome red brick house. Poor old aucuba has fallen out of favour in modern times and is much sneered at, which is a pity, for it

*POWIS CASTLE*
Top Terrace border

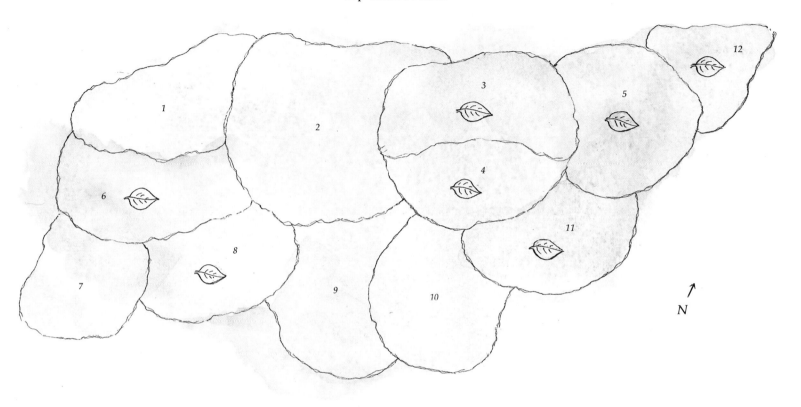

1. *Salvia mexicana*
2. *Cestrum parqui*
3. *Aralia elata* 'Variegata'
4. *Saxifrage*
5. *Melianthus major*
6. *Argyranthemum* 'Jamaica Primrose'
7. *Hebe* 'Alicia Amherst'
8. *Yucca recurvifolia*
9. *Osteospermum* 'Pink Whirls'
10. *Salvia microphylla neurepia*
11. *Yucca recurvifolia*
12. *Canna iridifolia*

DIMENSIONS: *10m×4.5m (15ft×33ft)*

is a handsome evergreen, particularly good in sunless city gardens where its glossy leaves, cheerfully freckled with gold, seem to withstand less-than-perfect conditions better than most. There are still about seventeen different varieties available, 'Crotonifolia' and 'Variegata' being the most popular. Only female clones will produce the scarlet berries which, while not essential, are a pleasant addition to the shrub's appearance during the winter.

At Peckover, the aucubas are interspersed with bushes of the golden privet, *Ligustrum ovalifolium* 'Aureum', and underplanted with ferns and a network of the attractive but rampant yellow dead nettle, *Lamiastrum galeobdolon*. Planted as a backdrop, the aucubas need something cool and unfussy in front of them – Japanese anemones, perhaps, or one of the white Rugosa roses such as 'Blanche Double de Coubert'.

Less familiar than the aucubas are the various kinds of variegated elder (*Sambucus nigra*). A creamy-white version, 'Albovariegata', won an Award of Merit from the Royal Horticultural Society as far back as 1897, but it has never been widely planted. It is now correctly known as *Sambucus nigra* 'Marginata' and makes a handsome shrub, easily kept to 1.8m/6ft in height, with creamy-white margins to all the leaves. 'Pulverulenta' is also variegated, but in a completely different way: all the leaves are streaked and marbled with white. It grows more slowly than 'Albovariegata'. Both thrive in some shade.

Mr Geoffrey Moon, the Head Gardener at WALLINGTON, has the National Collection of elders there and holds twenty-six varieties. As well as these two pale-leaved cultivars, he has the golden-variegated elder, *Sambucus nigra* 'Aureomarginata', which has leaves edged with a broad but irregular band of yellow. At Wallington this is under-planted with several bushes of a purple-leaved berberis. For the best foliage, you need to cut elders hard back in the spring. The disadvantage of this treatment is that you will have to sacrifice summer flowers and autumn berries. A compromise is possible. Cut out only one third of the old growth in rotation each spring and leave the rest to flower and fruit.

By the south drive at MONTACUTE, variegated hollies are used with purple cotinus and a foreground of catmint. In another purple and golden variegated scheme, hollies are partnered by purple nuts, regularly coppiced to give a plentiful supply of healthy new foliage. Golden-variegated euonymus fills in along the front.

## PERENNIALS FOR SMALLER SCHEMES

In smaller gardens, variegated herbaceous perennials will be more in demand than large shrubs such as elder and aucuba. A small garden brings its own problems. All plants must work hard for their keep. There will be no room in it for plants that are niggardly about paying their garden rent. Foliage plants are particularly good in this respect, since they give long-term form and substance to a small patch, which might otherwise be fussily crammed with flowers that leap into the limelight for three weeks at most and then sulk, with nothing to do for the rest of the year.

Particular care needs to be taken when using variegated plants in a small garden if the whole patch is not to look as though it has got a bad attack of some spotty rash. It is important that plant groups should be well composed so that there is not too much abrupt contrast. Variegated plants should be surrounded with others that are equivalent in colour tone: pale or greyish-green leaves, flowers with the same colour as the variegation. In this way you can create pools of light in a garden, softer and more pleasing than single, harsh spotlights. It is probably better to avoid wildly hectic plants such as *Tovara* 'Painter's Palette' and use instead pulmonarias, arums, hostas and the fine *Astrantia major* 'Sunningdale Variegated.' These are four of the best of a whole tribe of variegated plants that will thrive in fairly shady conditions, provided the shade is well fed and not dry.

Hostas, like snowdrops and the Arisaema family, attract fanatics. They are outstanding foliage plants, but the untramelled urge to collect them (there are at least 160 different kinds available in Britain) can result in tedious garden landscapes. Hostas have particularly easy-going genes,

*A national collection of elders has been established at Wallington and contains 26 different forms. This is* Sambucus nigra *'Marginata', one of several variegated kinds.*

which, with a little 'pimping' by plant-breeders, have produced a wide range of leaf colours in the genus. Between the extremes of bluish and yellowish, there are countless variations on the variegated theme. As a broad general rule of thumb, varieties with white variegation associate best with pink and mauve in cool planting schemes. Yellow variegated hostas combine with orange day-lilies, lysimachia or solidaster to give warm (not to say hot) effects.

The large leaves of hostas used in the foreground of a planting scheme with something feathery such as astilbe or fern behind, create a useful optical illusion in a small garden. They alter the perspective and make the plot seem deeper than it really is. Bright colours in the foreground, with dim shadowy ones especially blues behind, will have the same effect. Finding the right place for some hostas is complicated by the fact that certain types change colour as the season advances. *H. fortunei* 'Albopicta' begins spectacularly in spring with bright buttery leaves edged with green. By midseason, it is decidedly less painted. The middle fades and the edge darkens until the leaf is two-tone green, pleasant, but a good deal quieter than it was at its jazzy début. At POWIS CASTLE it makes a good show on the apple slope terrace, together with another hosta, 'Thomas Hogg', and the soft yellow leaves of the dead nettle *Lamium maculatum* 'Aureum.' *H. sieboldiana* 'Frances Williams' has bold corrugated leaves of glaucous blue-green. When they open they are edged with buff which intensifies through summer to quite a bright yellow. *H. elata* 'Aureomarginata' is also indecisive. It begins in spring as an extrovert with brightly yellow-edged leaves and then drifts into introversion as the yellow fades to white. 'Resonance', a newly introduced variety, has lance-shaped leaves and consistent foliage heavily margined in cream. The flowers are deep mauve.

Many of the herbaceous plants that we use in the garden tend to have the same rounded, hummocky profile: cranesbill, astrantia, alchemilla, epimedium. The sword-like leaves of plants such as iris and sisyrinchium provide a sharp contrast to this potentially soporific outlook of low hills. The native *Iris foetidissima* has a variegated cousin with leaves striped in cream and grey-green, which will grow happily in the same shady – even dry – conditions as the plain green kind. The flowers are a muddy mauve and insignificant, but the foliage lasts all the year round. *Iris pallida* 'Variegata' has even better foliage, boldly striped in blue-green and white. It also has better flowers of lavender blue, but it needs sun and dies down in winter. Both grow to about 450mm/18in.

*The strangely painted leaves, each tipped with bright pink and white, of the climber* Actinidia kolomikta. *A spiky agave is planted in the pot above.*

If you have a stream or a pond, you could do as Mr. Peter Hall, Head Gardener at DUNHAM MASSEY, has done and use the variegated flag iris *Iris pseudacorus* 'Variegata' by the water's edge with cimicifuga, astilbe and peltiphyllum. All these have good, strong foliage and the tall yellow striped leaves of the iris provide an excellent contrast with the feathery foliage of cimicifuga and astilbe and the big round umbrella leaves of the peltiphyllum.

Small variegated plants can also make useful edgings, particularly where the neighbouring planting is rather plain. A very good form of the dead nettle, *Lamiastrum galeobdolon* 'Silver Carpet' with silvery leaves netted in green, is used at POWIS CASTLE to fill in the dead ground between stone steps and the base of a dark yew hedge. *Sedum kamtschaticum* 'Variegatum' makes a neat edging, no more than 75mm/3in high, and has fleshy rosettes of green and white leaves, flushed with pink. In summer, the clusters of buds explode into star-shaped flowers of yellow and orange.

## CATALOGUE OF PLANTS

### Astrantia major 'Sunningdale Variegated'
*Deciduous perennial   Height and spread 600 × 600mm/2 × 2ft*
Used with some dark-leaved companion, perhaps candytuft or the purple foliage of *Viola labradorica purpurea*, this handsome astrantia, if grown in shade, gives pleasure for at least six months of the year. (By October it is looking distinctly shabby and it is best to take off the worst leaves then, leaving the rest as protection until spring.) The hand-shaped leaves are splashed heavily with yellow and cream and the flowers are similar to those of an ordinary astrantia, formal, papery ruffs of pale green and white. It is unfussy about soil but may lose its variegated markings if planted in full sun. It is excellent used as an underplanting for some rather sober shrub such as arbutus or a purple-leaved elder.

### Cornus alba (Dogwood)
*Deciduous shrub   Height and spread 2.4 × 3.9m/8 × 13ft*
'Elegantissima' has leaves broadly edged with white. 'Spaethii' has yellow-margined leaves. Both are useful, undemanding shrubs which quickly spread to make a thicket of stems. In winter the bark stands out, smooth and red. It is fully hardy and will grow on a wide variety of soils, acid or alkaline, waterlogged or dry. Use in full sun or medium shade. In deep shade, growth will be lax. Cut back hard in early spring to encourage new growth which will have larger leaves and brighter bark than that borne on old branches. Easy to control and elegant to look at.

### Cotoneaster horizontalis 'Variegatus'
*Deciduous shrub   Height and spread 300mm × 1.5m/1 × 5ft*
This is a form of the well-known herringbone cotoneaster. It does not flower or fruit as freely as its plain-leaved cousin, nor is it as vigorous, but it is as attractive in its ground-hugging form and very much more stylish in leaf. These are light grey-green, with cream margins, outlined in deep pink. It is unfussy about soil and will succeed in sun or shade. It will not tolerate being overlaid by the leaves of neighbouring plants and protests by dropping its own leaves instantly. It looks lovely with scillas in spring and provides a leavening foreground to some rather plain-leaved shrub such as *Hydrangea aspera villosa*. Use it at the front of a border where it can stretch out (but slowly) on to a stone-flagged path, or against a reasonably sunny wall, where the branches will be as happy pinned to a vertical as they are on the horizontal.

### Eryngium variifolium
*Evergreen perennial   Height and spread 450 × 300mm/18 × 12in*
The spiny green leaves, veined in white, make a handsome rosette which sits close to the ground and is especially valuable in winter. The thistle-flowers, though not as good as others in this family, are worth having and last from midsummer to early autumn. It grows best in

*The spiky toothed leaves of* **Eryngium variifolium** *conspicuously veined with white.*

deep, well-drained soil in full sun. An autumn
mulch around the crown of leaves will pay
dividends the following year. At ICKWORTH these
eryngiums are used in the big flower border that
curves round the oval lawn to the north of the
house. The colour scheme is purple, blue, white
and pale yellow: catmint, achillea, acanthus,
variegated philadelphus, echinops, cotinus and
monkshood (*Aconitum napellus*).

### Felicia amelloides 'Variegata'

*Evergreen sub-shrub    Height and spread 450 ×
225mm/18 × 9in*

This is a very showy, though tender, South
African plant, particularly good for pots, either on
its own or mixed with heliotrope or lobelia. It also
looks lovely bedded out round standards of some
tall filigree-leaved shrub such as *Artemisia
arborescens*. The felicia has small spoon-shaped
leaves in cream and pale green. Fairly late in the
summer it starts throwing up bright blue daisy-
flowers, each on a long, thin stem. Though it is a
good spreader, it is not hardy. Plants in pots can
be moved inside to overwinter, or softwood
cuttings can be taken in July and August. Give it
full sun and well-drained soil. In the favoured
south-west of the country, plants may overwinter
successfully out of doors. At KILLERTON, this
felicia is dramatically combined with the black
grassy leaves of ophiopogon.

### Fuchsia magellanica

*Deciduous shrub    Height and spread 1.2 × 1.5m/4 ×
5ft*

'Variegata' has grey-green leaves margined with
white. 'Tricolor' has silver-grey foliage,
irregularly splashed with green. New growths are
suffused with pink and purple. Although that
may sound over-complicated, the overall effect is
restful, and a good foil for the scarlet and purple
flowers which cover the bush from high summer
until the first frosts. In hard winters, all top
growth will be cut back to the base, but even the
harsh conditions of winter 1986-7 did not kill
these fuchsias outright. They will thrive in any
soil, acid or alkaline, and although they prefer full

*Our native evergreen holly has many boldly variegated forms, both silver and gold. Though slow growing, the
foliage provides year round furnishing in town and country gardens.*

sun, will also give a decent performance in light shade. Occasionally, shoots of the variegated varieties will revert to plain green, and these must be pruned out immediately. For an extremely cool combination, use with the prostrate shrub rose 'Raubritter' which has old-fashioned, cup-shaped, double flowers of pink. Tall galtonias also look good with either 'Variegata' or 'Tricolor' fuchsias.

### Ilex (Holly)
*Evergreen shrub or tree   Height and spread 3.9 × 2.4m/13 × 8ft*
One of the relatively few native evergreens, holly is a much undervalued garden plant. It is too slow-growing for those who want their gardens to materialize like a pop-up picture book. But like the equally unfashionable heroes of Edwardian novels, holly is staunch, hardy, handsome in an understated way and always there when other flashier subjects have shot their bolt and disappeared. Varietal names are decidedly obtuse. 'Golden King' is female, 'Golden Queen' and 'Silver Queen' are male. Only female forms bear berries, but male trees are essential for effective pollination. There are about thirty different variegated kinds, which can be roughly divided into warm gold and cooler silver. Varieties of *I. × altaclerensis* have wide, smooth, relatively unprickly leaves as in 'Golden King', which has leaves edged in bright yellow, or 'Silver Sentinel', which has mottled leaves with creamy edges. The hedgehog holly (*Ilex aquifolium* 'Ferox') is smaller than most, rarely more than

1.8m/6ft high or wide at maturity. It has double rations of prickles. The leaves are slightly twisted with spines erupting from the leaf surfaces as well as surrounding the edges. *Ilex a.* 'Ferox Argentea' has hedgehog leaves margined in white, and *I.a.* 'Ferox Aurea' is variegated with gold.

### Salvia officinalis (Sage)
*Evergreen shrub   Height and spread 900mm × 1.2m/3 × 4ft*
'Icterina' is a soft, yellow, variegated version of the common kitchen sage; 'Tricolor' a more complicated combination of green leaves with white edges, the new growth flushed pink and purple. The latter is a weak grower and not reliably hardy. Both are best in full sun and both make attractive low dividing hedges in ornamental vegetable gardens. All sages benefit by having their new growth cut back by half in spring. This prevents them from becoming woody and lax in growth. At KILLERTON yellow 'Icterina' is grouped with osteospermum and the grey downy leaves of *Euryops pectinatus* which enjoys the same sunny position and well-drained soil as the sage.

### Scrophularia auriculata 'Variegata' (Figwort)
*Deciduous perennial   Height and spread 600 × 450mm/2ft × 18in*
This is an outstanding plant for reasonably moist soil. It has oval, toothed leaves which are dark green, brightly variegated with cream. The maroon flowers produced in July and August are scarcely worth bothering about and can be

pinched out as they appear, to encourage the plant to concentrate on the leaf display. Although it is generally thought of as a plant for half shade, it is spectacularly used in full sun in the border of the orangery terrace at POWIS. Bright blue tradescantia and orange day-lilies are its companions here. It also looks good with dark blue delphiniums behind it and small yellow day-lilies alongside. At WALLINGTON, the scrophularia is teamed with grey-blue *Salvia sclarea turkestanica* and the spherical purple flower-heads of *Allium christophii*.

### Symphytum × uplandicum 'Variegatum' (Comfrey)
*Deciduous perennial   Height and spread 900 × 600mm/3 × 2ft*
This is a superb, eye-catching plant, not the slightest bit refined and not ashamed of it either. The leaves are large – up to 300mm/1ft long – grey-green with a wide margin of cream, which fade to white as the leaves age. It clumps up rather slowly, but does best in moist, rich ground in half shade (full sun may scorch the pale leaves). In early summer it throws up a tall flowering stem covered with hairy pink and blue tubular flowers, and consequently the leaves go to pieces. As soon as you are tired of the flowering stem, cut it off, shear back the old basal leaves and this comfrey will reward you by growing a fine new crop of leaves which are not disfigured by any further flowering. Delicate plants will be completely cowed by it. Give it robust neighbours, or grow it in isolation against some plain, dark background.

# COLOURED FOLIAGE

Twopence coloured is not necessarily better than penny plain when it comes to choosing foliage plants for the garden. Purple, gold and silver leaves make for a rich diet, as indigestible as caviar if ladled on too thick. To use the full palette, you need the kind of space that Leopold de Rothschild had at ASCOTT in Buckinghamshire. In 1874, he laid out an exuberant Victorian garden here with the help of the famous nursery, James Veitch and Sons of Chelsea. At Ascott, coloured foliage runs riot. There is golden elm, golden privet, golden holly, golden cedar. There are blue larches, junipers, silver willow, purple berberis, cotinus, prunus, sycamore and copper beech. There is a great deal of topiary, usually in golden box and yew, including an extremely complicated sundial with a bi-coloured centre-piece, golden yew on top of green. The numbers are green, but a quotation, 'Light and shade by turn, but love always', is painstakingly clipped out of golden yew. It is all extremely theatrical, very showy and impossible to emulate unless you have at least thirty acres to play with. If Mr Rothschild had been able to find purple, silver and gold grass, doubtless he

*Two views of the splendidly planted garden at Ascott, where coloured foliage runs riot. The view to the fountain (above) is framed in clipped balls of golden yew. The sundial (opposite) has numbers of plain green but the motto around it is painstakingly clipped from golden yew.*

would have used that too, but the vast expanse of undemanding green that laps around this psychedelic collection of trees and shrubs is an indispensable foil, as necessary as a straight man is to a comic. Jammed together in a small garden without the buffer of the plain grass, this sort of unrestrained planting would not be a success.

## THE COLOUR PURPLE
Of the three, purple foliage is perhaps the most difficult to place. It looks lovely in spring, particularly on copper beech or purple *Cotinus coggygria* when the young leaves have a bronze translucence about them. The colour can seem heavy and dead as summer wears on, however, and in a big mass,

*The mealy-textured foliage of* **Vitis vinifera** *'Purpurea', an excellent foliage climber for wall or pergola.*
*Early flowering clematis can be run through it to give variety at the beginning of the season.*

particularly, as with the beech or the sycamore, it can be overwhelming. In winter, most of the purples lose their leaves. Only a few, such as the hebes 'Autumn Glory' and 'Purple Queen' and the low-growing purple sage will have anything to contribute after autumn. Shrubs such as cotinus, berberis and the purple nut, *Corylus maxima* 'Purpurea', are likely to be the most useful in the average garden as they all respond well to heavy pruning. This stimulates them to produce fresh growths of good new leaves and also stops them taking up too much space.

In the big borders of the Trust gardens, cotinus is often used as a recurring motif, like the pattern on a wallpaper. This breaks up the length into sectors that the eye can encompass all at once and imposes a pattern on what otherwise might be rather an unmanageable bulk. In a smaller garden, different stratagems are called for and the cotinus will more likely become the centrepiece of a planting group, probably of silver, blue and pink. You cannot go wrong with silver, blue and pink and often that is precisely what is wrong with the scheme. It is too predictable. It takes more courage to use yellow and orange with purple, but the rewards are correspondingly greater – if the plan comes off. It may end in disaster, but there is always another year.

The most useful borders from a plagiarist's point of view are those where a small section can be abstracted from the whole without losing any of its potency in the process. If you are wanting to create a strong foliage border with purple as the dominant theme, you could scarcely do better than to steal some ideas from Mrs Phyllis Reiss's fine west border in the cedar court at TINTINHULL. Purple berberis and the golden-variegated dogwood *Cornus alba* 'Spaethii' are the twin lynchpins of this border. Three purple-leaved plums, *Prunus* × *blireana*, *P. cerasifera*, and *P.* × *cistena* provide the rest of the main framework. The skill lies in the choice of companions to fill in the middle and bottom layers of the planting. Pink roses are effective here: the Hybrid Musk 'Cornelia', the China 'Fellenberg', the Floribunda 'Rosemary Rose' and the Bourbon 'Zéphirine Drouhin'. *Rosa glauca* is

*The superb glossy leaves of a purple aeonium at Overbecks. Though tender, these are excellent planted in pots and overwintered under cover.*

used as much for its blue-grey leaves as for its flowers. The rare *Berberis temolaica*, introduced from the Temo-la pass in north-west China, has similar pewter-coloured foliage. Solomon's seal arches gracefully in front of the berberis and on the lowest level variegated periwinkle and dead nettle weave their way round the taller shrubs. The fleshy *Sedum telephium maximum* 'Atropurpureum' and grey-leaved lamb's ear are used in pools along the front of the border with occasional sheaves of *Veronica austriaca teucrium*. There is more – tall eupatorium, bronze stands of fennel, prostrate juniper – but by combining some of these ingredients, the thoughtful gardener will be able to create a Reissian border of great panache.

The smoke bush, cotinus, is perhaps the single most useful shrub among the purples. In summer it is surrounded by a haze of the diaphanous flowers that give it its common name. Its simple, rounded leaves are particularly pleasing and provide an excellent foil for foreground planting. (This should *not* be artemisia, if you have an ounce of individuality in you. That particular purple and grey combo has become one of the most overworked in the canon.) At LYTES CARY big, blowzy pink opium poppies are used to great effect in front of cotinus. Both flower and leaves, the latter a fleshy, glaucous colour, contrast well with the matt purple of the cotinus behind. At BARRINGTON COURT the cotinus are pollarded every year in October or November to encourage plentiful supplies of new leaves. In the border outside the lily garden, a large specimen is teamed with meadowsweet and both kinds of acanthus – the cabbagy-leaved *A. mollis* and the more finely cut *A. spinosus*.

Cotinus is particularly good if you can plant it against the light. The leaves change to a marvellous translucent amber when the sun shines through them. The plain foliage contrasts well with an underplanting of something fussier like *Cotoneaster horizontalis* with its tiny leaves. At WALLINGTON, the yellow trumpet flowers of *Lilium pyrenaicum* combine dramatically with the foliage of *Cotinus coggygria* 'Foliis Purpureis', more bronze than purple, despite its name.

In the small, walled courtyard in front of the sixteenth-century manor house at TRERICE, the two facing borders have a purple and gold theme. In the east border, the elegant *Abutilon × suntense* is used with purple berberis, under-planted with lavender. The showy variegated *Buddleja* 'Harlequin' with rich purple flowers stands behind another purple-leaved berberis, with a large clump of *Sedum telephium* 'Variegatum' taking up the foreground. A fig trained flat against the wall has the deep purple-flowered *Clematis × jackmanii* running through it with pale yellow *Argyranthemum* 'Jamaica Primrose' planted at its feet. Purple-leaved cotinus is paired with the low-growing *Anthemis* 'Mrs E.C. Buxton', grey, ferny foliage with pale yellow daisy-flowers floating on top. On this side the emphasis is on purple with touches of gold.

*Purple* Cotinus coggygria *provides strong foliage contrast in the rock garden at Sizergh Castle.*

## TRERICE
### Yellow and purple border

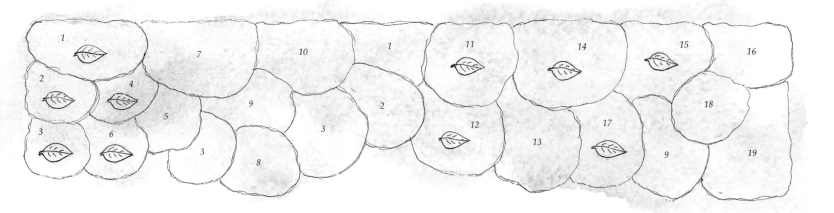

1. *Ajuga reptans* 'Atropurpurea'
2. *Philadelphus coronarius* 'Aureus'
3. *Tovara virginiana* 'Painter's Palette'
4. *Euonymus fortunei* 'Emerald 'n' Gold'
5. *Hypericum kouytchense*
6. *Ficus carica*
7. *Aster amellus* 'Violet Queen'
8. *Clematis × jackmanii*
9. Delphinium (blue)
10. *Digitalis ferruginea*
11. *Anthemis tinctoria*
12. *Cotinus coggygria* 'Royal Purple'
13. *Solanum crispum*
14. *Euphorbia polychroma*
15. *Lavandula* 'Hidcote'
16. *Ceratostigma willmottianum*
17. *Tovara virginiana* 'Painter's Palette'
18. Hypericum
19. *Corokia × virgata*

N

DIMENSIONS: *14m×2.3m (46ft×7.8ft)*

*The bronze foliage of the annual dahlia 'Redskin' makes an important contribution to the success of this planting scheme at Overbecks.*

On the west side, the combination is reversed. A golden-leaved philadelphus is partnered by low bushes of a golden-variegated euonymus, with the vividly painted leaves of tovara alongside. A plain philadelphus has the vivid spiraea 'Goldflame' in front of it. The new foliage of this spiraea is apricot-coloured when it first unfurls in spring. It gradually changes to an orange-red and finally settles down to gold. The pink flowers in midsummer are rather an embarrassment against this background, but if you are offended by such solecisms you can cut them off. The foliage is excellent, though may scorch in strong sunlight. Hard pruning in spring will encourage fresh supplies of good leaves.

In another grouping, the golden-leaved *Fuchsia* 'Golden Thumb' is used with a leathery-leaved pittosporum, a purple cotinus and a frothy front planting of coronilla, which has tiny leaves of rich glaucous green. The fine shrubby St John's wort, *Hypericum* 'Rowallane', has a golden-variegated sedum at its feet and artemisia and 'Hidcote' lavender to the side.

## YELLOW AND GOLD

Gold foliage is often less stable an element than purple. The leaves of *Philadelphus coronarius* 'Aureus' start out a promising gold in spring but fade to a much less inspiring pale green as the season advances. The golden berberis, *Berberis thunbergii* 'Aurea', does the same thing. So does the elder, *Sambucus nigra* 'Aurea'. This is no reason not to plant them. The philadelphus, for instance, as strongly scented as the old-fashioned varieties, looks superb in spring under a big cherry such as 'Tai-haku'. The cherry's leaves are rich bronze when they first open up and this contrasts most agreeably with the then quite vivid leaves of the philadelphus. At DUNHAM MASSEY it is used in front of a young cercidiphyllum, whose new foliage is also flushed with bronze-red.

The soft golden foliage of gleditsia or the golden maple, *Acer shirasawanum* 'Aureum', has a tendency to scorch in full sun. This makes it look very sick and uncomfortable. Different plants have quite specific needs and it is worth

*Exotic foliage plants flourish in the shelter of the conservatory at Wallington,*
*where coleus, ficus, palms and feathery acacias crowd together on the staging.*

checking on these before you consign a plant to a certain position in the garden. Although it may shortly be overtaken by the newly introduced golden-leaved birch, *Robinia pseudoacacia* 'Frisia' has been one of the most commonly planted, golden-foliage trees of the last few years, but probably less than half will grow to maturity. It looks deceptively fragile and dainty in the nursery or garden centre, but is actually a sport of a tree that can easily top 9m/30ft. As it is a relatively recent introduction, nobody knows yet what height it will eventually reach, but certainly some front gardens are going to be too small to contain it. Robinia also has particularly brittle wood, so that branches are prone to snap or split if it is planted in an exposed position. In the right place, it is an outstanding foliage tree, the colour clear and bright, the leaves like short strings of flat beads. It is best planted on its own, rather than hemmed in in a mixed planting. If you can arrange a dark background for it, so much the better. Plain ivy would be good.

Although yellow is shunned by some extremely finely tuned gardeners, it is a cheerful colour to have about, which is perhaps why the golden robinia has been so successful. Gold foliage placed in a gloomy corner of the garden can transform it from a pit of despair into a place of pilgrimage. Golden privet is a particularly useful member of the sweetness and light school as it is evergreen. Privet generally has been despised for decades as suburban, but the golden form, *Ligustrum ovalifolium* 'Aureum', is in all senses an eye-opener. It is perfectly happy in sun or shade, and it is particularly pleasing combined with clumps of the easy-going but invaluable alchemilla, which has sprays of lime-green flowers. Regale lilies added to this group would make it something that even the most picky gardener could not sneer at. At ASCOTT golden privet is used with a tall feathery bamboo and the giant rhubarb leaves of *Rheum palmatum* to make a bold planting of well-contrasted foliage.

*The golden foliage of an elder* Sambucus laciniata *'Aurea' silhouetted against a billowing hedge of yew at Powis Castle.*

## SILVER, GREY AND BLUE

Where gold foliage warms up a scene, grey will cool it down. Silver and grey plants demand (and have had) whole books to themselves, so popular have they become. This popularity is a puzzle, since so many of the group come from hot Mediterranean regions where the colour and texture of their leaves has come about as a natural adaptation to drought conditions. That is not what they are most likely to find in the British Isles, where damp will probably be their chief enemy. Nor is the dull, matt texture of their leaves the most heartwarming thing to come across on the sort of dull, matt day that our climate excels in.

There has been, in recent years, a great vogue for all-grey gardens, brought about perhaps by the great success of the white garden at SISSINGHURST. To buy a bumper bundle of greys and then plant them all together may on the surface seem to be a foolproof way of creating a well-coordinated garden, but, paradoxically, it is not. An all-grey garden is a difficult thing to do well and too often has all the allure of a collection of dirty washing-up cloths. Many of the greys – santolina, artemisia, helichrysum – have the same dull texture, determined by the tiny hairs that cover the surface of their foliage and give it its grey colouring. By using greys all together, you may lose not only contrasts of colour, but contrasts of texture as well. The temptation to lump them together is increased by the fact that many of the herbaceous kinds need the same sort of growing conditions: well-drained soil that is not too rich. Unless you are an extremely confident stage-manager of your garden, it will be easier to use greys in contrast with other foliage and in mixed borders of herbaceous perennials. If you are determined to proceed with a grey/white scheme, then it is wise to go and absorb the juxtapositions of a really good piece of planting before you leap to the task. The small fountain garden at TINTINHULL may provide a better template than the better-known white garden at Sissinghurst.

At Tintinhull small standard trees of an unusual willow, *Salix helvetica*, are used as the centrepieces of each of the four small triangular beds that surround the pool and fountain. The leaves of this little tree are an intense pewter-grey, with white undersides, and are small and narrow, like those of most of this family; but the tree is slow-growing and can easily be kept in a neat shape by pruning in early spring. Off-white iris, stained with mauve, forms a successful contrast with the elegant steel-blue grass *Helictotrichon sempervirens*. Neat mounds of santolina offset plantings of white mallow and campanula, while grey mats of the fine-leaved *Anthemis cupaniana* sprawl over the front of the paving. Galtonias, which have tall hyacinth-spires of white flowers in late summer, are interplanted with the white-flowered *Lychnis coronaria alba*. This is an excellent perennial with lance-shaped leaves that combine to make bold, slightly crinkled clumps of foliage. They are very handsome even without the flowers that last throughout the summer. Artemisia and white colchicums underplant bushes of the roses 'Iceberg' and 'Margaret Merril'.

Their slightly exotic, foreign air makes the greys ideal plants to use in containers. They can also withstand some slight drying out better than native species. Some, such as artemisia and cineraria, have a filigree, ethereal quality that makes an ideal contrast to a rather more prosaic floral companion such as petunia. Others, such as helichrysum, are tender and so are only suitable for summer shows. Helichrysum, either the silver or the lime, grows at a prodigious rate but is not a swamper. Its habit of growth is elegant, and from a largish pot, it will hang down and reach out until it has made a wide skirt of handsome foliage which almost obscures the pot itself. It is a favourite of Mr Jimmy Hancock, the Head Gardener at POWIS CASTLE, who uses it in the magnificent basketweave terracotta pots that line the

*The famous white garden at Sissinghurst with the weeping silver-leaved pear* Pyrus salicifolia *'Pendula' closing the vista at the end of the path. Clumps of artemisia echo the foliage theme and carpets of evergreen* Lamium maculatum album *fill in at ground level.*

orangery terrace at Powis. Fuchsias and trailing blue lobelia are its usual partners here. The lime-coloured *Helichrysum petiolare* 'Limelight' is happy in half shade, in fact it is better there than in full sun which tends to scorch the leaves. At OVERBECKS, it makes a magnificent companion for spiky, dark-leaved phormiums.

One of the staunchest of the greys is catmint, either the exuberant 'Six Hills Giant' or the more restrained 'Little Titch'. Purists may complain that catmint is not a real grey. Certainly, against artemisias and senecios it may look quite green, but it is always the grey side of green and, being fully hardy, is a great deal easier to manage than some of the true greys. Being a herbaceous perennial, it can be cut back to the ground in late autumn and will refresh itself each spring with long aromatic sprays of grey-green foliage, topped with toning grey-blue flowers. Brave gardeners cut it hard back after its first flush of flower to keep its foliage looking fresh and give a seond flush of flower in late summer. It makes a fine edging for paths and is beautifully used in this way at TINTINHULL, where it lines both sides of the long central walk leading through the vegetable garden. Lavender is the traditional choice for this position but is much more difficult to keep in good shape than catmint. If not clipped over carefully in the spring, lavender quickly becomes woody and leggy. Catmint is also used to edge the front of the herbaceous border at OXBURGH, where it provides a fine, soft foil for *Hemerocallis lilio-asphodelus*, *Aruncus dioicus*, *Rudbeckia* 'Goldsturm' and the pyrethrum 'Eileen May Robinson'. Pink flowers seem to be the usual companions for catmint, but it is marvellous with yellow, too. At THE COURTS it is used to fill in under the topiary globes of golden yew in the forecourt, where its soft indeterminate colour provides exactly the right contrast with the more strident presence of the yew. It is equally good with purple foliage, used as it is at LYTES CARY in front of a large bush of cotinus, with a cream shrub rose as a buffer. In the same border here, it is grouped with purple berberis and low mounds of purple sage.

Blue foliage is actually closer to grey than blue but is often distinguished by a waxy sheen, the glaucous finish that gives the leaves of rue or eucalyptus their distinctive appearance. It is a colour that you often find in the large family of conifers, whether a giant such as *Cedrus atlantica glauca* or a prostrate pygmy juniper. The eucalyptus' leaves are most blue in the rounded juvenile foliage. Adult leaves change shape as well as colour, hanging down in long, grey-blue sickles rather than clasping the stem as the young leaves do. Regular hard pruning will ensure a constant supply of young leaves. There is a foreign look about eucalyptus that makes it difficult to place amongst native oaks and beeches, but they grow in groves to the east and west of the Italian garden at MOUNT STEWART, where exceptionally mild winters are normal.

*Othonnopsis cheirifolia* has equally arresting leaves – stiff, paddle-shaped and richly glaucous. It is a low, sprawling thing, never getting above 30cm (1ft) and covered with yellow daisies in June. It grows in the west-facing border against the house at KILLERTON with argyranthemum, *Convolvulus cneorum* and various diascias. These are all slightly tender, but the othonnopsis, having such extraordinarily good leaves, is worth risking, particularly in sheltered town gardens. Rue is probably the best known of the 'blue' foliage plants. It has a neat, bushy habit and small, rounded leaves. It is fully hardy, but likes a well-drained soil and as much sun as it can get. In summer it has mustard yellow flowers, not a great asset, but they are easily disposed of. The leaves have a bitter smell and can cause skin rashes. 'Jackman's Blue' is the best variety. It is used as a permanent filling in the parterre at OXBURGH HALL and makes a low hedge round beds in the parterre at MOUNT STEWART.

*Lavender and roses in the silver foliage border at Barrington Court. Russian sage (Perovskia atriplicifolia) and Artemisia ludoviciana emphasise the silver theme. The lavender needs clipping each spring to prevent it become leggy.*

## CATALOGUE OF PLANTS

### Artemisia
*Evergreen shrubs and deciduous perennials   Height and spread varies widely*

This is an invaluable family of plants which can provide a wide range of handsome grey foliage, low and finely cut as in *A. schmidtiana* or tall and relatively broad-leaved as in *A. × campestris borealis*. Many of the shrubby kinds look and behave like herbaceous perennials, but all of them like dry soils and brilliant drainage. One of the best of the tribe is *A.* 'Powis Castle', a shrubby, spreading plant that gets no taller than 600mm/2ft with beautiful, finely cut foliage. It makes no attempt to flower, which is a great advantage. With a few honourable exceptions (such as *A. lactiflora* and *A.* 'Lambrook Silver'), artemisia flowers are often a grubby mistake. At POWIS CASTLE, where Mr Jimmy Hancock has made it a speciality, *Artemisia* 'Powis Castle' makes a fine edging under the great billowing bulwarks of yew on the top terrace. The taller *A.* 'Lambrook Silver' is also used in the borders here and on the orangery terrace is particularly striking paired with the bold, pinnate leaves of *Rodgersia pinnata* 'Superba'.

### Berberis thunbergii (Barberry)
*Deciduous shrub   Height and spread 1.8 × 1.2m/6 × 4ft (depending on variety)*

'Atropurpurea' is the standard variety with rich purple leaves that colour red in autumn. 'Atropurpurea Nana' is a dwarf cousin, only 600 × 450mm/2ft × 18in. The rest come somewhere between these two extremes of height and spread. 'Rose Glow' has leaves mottled with pink and 'Helmond Pillar' is useful where you want a tall, thin pillar of purple. Although 1.2m/4ft high, this variety is only about 450mm/18in across. All varieties are easy to grow and will tolerate less than perfect soils. Pruning is not essential, but straggly growths can be cut back hard in February and old stems taken out at ground level if the shrub is getting out of bounds. At THE COURTS purple berberis is beautifully set off against the fine leaves of a maple, *Acer griseum*. At MONTACUTE dark berberis provides the background for the fresh green leaves and paper-white flowers of the rose 'Blanche Double de Coubert'. Pale blue iris complete the picture.

### Cimicifuga ramosa 'Atropurpurea' (Bugbane)
*Deciduous perennial   Height and spread 1.8m × 900mm/6 × 3ft*

As its name suggests, 'Atropurpurea' should be dark blackish-purple throughout. Plants offered by nurseries are often raised from seed and are not dark enough to deserve the name. At its best it is an invaluable, tall, late-flowering plant for the mixed border. The purple foliage is light and ferny, each leaf being made up from ten to twelve leaflets. They are easy in moist, well-fed soil, but resent being poked about by over-zealous gardeners. Cut down stems in November; mulch plants well in March. They do not require much more. This variety has stems and leaves covered with a deep purple bloom and long poker-spires of creamy flowers. At OVERBECKS it is combined with the dainty, orange-yellow spikes of *Kniphofia galpinii*. At POWIS it is used with clumps of *Francoa sonchifolia*, one of those plants that *cognoscenti* rave about and non-gardeners take for an unfamiliar kind of dock. In another group at Powis, it is put with white mallows and the pale daisy-flowers of *Argyranthemum* 'Jamaica Primrose'.

### Eucalyptus (Gum tree)
*Evergreen tree   Height and spread at least 9.6 × 3.9m/32 × 13ft*

Local conditions will dictate which of this large and handsome family of trees you can grow. All have good blue-grey glaucous foliage, which changes dramatically as the tree ages. Juvenile foliage is usually rounded, adult leaves long and thin. If left to itself, eucalyptus will grow as a tall, narrow single-stemmed tree. You can, however, keep it as a low multi-stemmed shrub by pruning it hard, or coppicing it in early spring. This will also have a Dorian Gray effect on the foliage which will never change to its mature form. Useful work is being done by breeders to select seed from clones which survive in the wild in less than comfortable conditions, which should produce trees hardier than those now generally available. All are sparse, spare trees. *Eucalyptus gunnii* is reckoned to be one of the toughest. All eucalypts should be planted as small seedlings and not staked. Larger plants are unlikely to make trees and are inclined to topple especially if they are given support in early life.

### Filipendula ulmaria 'Aurea' (Meadowsweet)
*Deciduous perennial   Height and spread 900 × 600mm/3 × 2ft*

Moist, well-fed soil is essential to get the best performance from this handsome, golden-leaved perennial. It also needs light shade, for the soft pinnate leaves scorch badly in full sun. This plant can only cope with one thing at a time and the effort of flowering has a disastrous effect on the leaves. Much better to remove the flower-spikes as they are not wildly exciting and keep up the supply of well-coloured leaves. In deep shade the yellow will fade to green. Mulch established plants with compost or manure in April/May and cut down all stems in late October. It is used dramatically in the stream garden at DUNHAM MASSEY, close to the water where its companions are *Euphorbia palustris*, the skunk cabbage (*Lysichiton americanus*) and the white *Astilbe* 'Deutschland'.

### Melianthus major
*Semi-evergreen sub-shrub   Height and spread 1.2 × 1.2m/4 × 4ft*

If this plant were not so doubtfully hardy, you would see it in every garden you visit, for it is an outstanding foliage plant. It has terrific style, an architectural shape overall, stupendous leaves of a steely blue-green and waxy texture. Once established, it will survive zero temperatures. The problem lies in getting it through its first few winters. Protecting the crowns with bracken or straw may help. It is seen at its best in the gardens of the south-west where, as it is not butchered every winter, it can grow up to 3m/10ft tall. In a region where it has to start from scratch each spring, it will not reach beyond 1.2m/4ft. At TRENGWAINTON it is used with tree peonies and the handsome fern *Polystichum setiferum* to make an extremely elegant group. In another planting here, you can see it with olearia and hefty clumps of echium. Easier to emulate in less favoured gardens is the combination at PENRHYN: melianthus with the bronze-red foliage of photinia.

*Melianthus,* **Stachys byzantina,** *santolina and purple-leaved berberis.*

### Robinia pseudoacacia 'Frisia' (False acacia)

*Deciduous tree    Height and spread 6 × 3.9m/ 20 × 13ft*

Although it is very late to break into leaf, this is a valuable foliage tree, with gleaming, pinnate leaves, bright yellow, which do not fade to green as some other gold-leaved shrubs do. Because it is fast growing, the wood tends to be brittle, so it should be given a place sheltered from the prevailing wind. As the tree matures, the bark becomes as furrowed as a drunkenly ploughed field. The foliage stands out best against a plain, dark background. In a town courtyard it will shine against a wall of ivy, partnered perhaps by the handsome evergreen mahonia 'Charity', which will come into bloom as the robinia is losing its leaves. It will thrive in any soil, acid or alkaline, but is better in sun than shade.

### Romneya coulteri (Tree poppy)

*Deciduous sub-shrub    Height and spread 900mm × 1.8m/3 × 6ft*

This Californian native makes a handsome feature, either standing on its own, or combined with other plants in a mixed border. At DUNSTER, it is elegantly used with clumps of blue agapanthus to make a fine late-summer show. It is not strictly a foliage plant, as it bears beautiful, large, white, papery poppy-flowers. It has found a place here because the leaves are so handsome: deeply lobed and cut, a glaucous sea-green in colour. It is a maddening plant, however. In some gardens it romps like a weed, spreading and suckering from underground runners. In others it will not establish at all and sulks and dies in a season. It does not like being disturbed, so if you are one of the lucky ones for whom it will grow, leave it well alone.

### Ruta graveolens (Rue)

*Evergreen shrub    Height and spread 600 × 900mm/ 2 × 3ft*

'Jackman's Blue' is the best form of this neat shrub, which has small, deeply divided, fern-like leaves of a fine glaucous blue. It grows well in large tubs and makes an attractive loose mound, good placed on either side of a porch or entrance. It does best in a light, well-drained soil but is more tolerant than many other greys about where it will grow. A really severe frost may cut back the foliage, leaving it looking pale and withered, but this can easily be sheared off in early spring. The flowers are a slight embarrassment, a dirty mustard, but can be removed as well. It is lovely in spring set off by clear yellow tulips, perhaps 'Bellona' or 'Candela'. Later, it combines well with white mallows or the purple-blue flowers of hibiscus.

### Salvia officinalis 'Purpurascens' (Purple sage)

*Evergreen shrub    Height and spread 600 × 600mm/ 2 × 2ft*

This is a purple-leaved variant of the kitchen sage and is equally good for the pot. It looks tough but is not hardy in the very worst winters. Full sun and a well-drained soil will remind it of its southern European homeland. It can grow rather lax and woody if left to its own devices. A light clipping every spring will keep it shapely. The young foliage of this variety is a particular delight, a velvety purplish-grey. Being low-growing, it makes a useful front-of-border filler. In the walled garden at FELBRIGG, it grows in front of a tall, spiky cardoon and a fine specimen of the gold-leaved currant *Ribes alpinum* 'Aureum'. It also combines well with other front-row perennials such as *Viola cornuta*, blue or white, and the neat pink sprays of diascia.

### Tanacetum parthenium 'Aureum' (Golden feverfew)

*Semi-evergreen perennial    Height and spread 300 × 300mm/12 × 12in*

This is a short-lived perennial at best but is such an enthusiastic self-seeder that the problem will not be in keeping it, but in curbing it. On dull foggy days in November the low mounds of rich, yellow foliage shine out like beacons. It is undemanding, which means that it is underrated, but particularly good among blue flowers and with the lime-green trumpets of tobacco flower. Its own single, white daisy-flowers are nothing to get excited about but can be sheared off if they dissipate the effect that you are after. Try it with Jacob's ladder (*Polemonium caeruleum*), campanulas and the dark-leaved *Viola labradorica purpurea*. It makes a neat edging and would be an excellent choice for a ribbon border, with alchemilla behind.

# FERNS, GRASSES AND BAMBOOS

Fashion is a fickle dictator and has been responsible for banishing several groups of plants that ought to be playing a greater part in today's gardens. Ferns, for instance, have never regained the popularity that they had in Victorian times, when different forms – crested, waved, tasselled, some frilled like parsley – were avidly collected and given totally unpronounceable names. The names may be the problem. *Athyrium filix-femina plumosum cristatum* is not a tag that trips lightly off the tongue. It is a lovely thing, though, one of the family known as lady ferns, growing about 900mm/3ft high with golden green fronds, crested at the top.

*The lady fern,* Athyrium filix-femina *(above) in the rock garden at Sizergh Castle where the National Trust has a large collection of ferns. Ferns are also used as a carpet in the woodland garden at Trelissick (opposite).*

Grasses, on the other hand, are very much in fashion, with new varieties being introduced each season from New Zealand and Japan. The flowering varieties are particularly valuable in autumn and early winter when the stems make elegant fountains of buff and cream. They are possibly easier to use in mixed plantings than ferns, which generally demand the sort of cool, shaded conditions that you find under north walls or in woodland. The monster grasses, bamboos, have a fine champion in Christopher Lloyd, who uses them imaginatively in mixed plantings at his garden, Great Dixter in Sussex, but his is still a voice crying in the wilderness. Tall varieties are occasionally recommended as quick-growing screens to hide eyesores, but they can do much more than that. Rampant *Sinarundinaria nitida* has perhaps given the whole tribe a bad name, but not all are tall, nor are they necessarily invasive. All three – ferns, grasses and bamboos – are valuable foliage plants, and can be used either in groups on their own, as underplanting, or combined in mixed borders.

## FERNS

At THE COURTS, the Gardener-in-charge, Mr Andrew Humphris, has made a fine sunken garden using ferns and bamboo. It lies on the left-hand side of the main entrance into the garden and surrounds an irregularly shaped pond, roughly 1.2m/4ft wide and four times as long. The whole thing is contained in a space about 10.5×9m/35 × 30ft, with a path running round close to the pond and one long bed raised up alongside the path. Big clumps of *Arundinaria nitida* provide screens on two sides of the pond, with the oak-leaved *Hydrangea quercifolia* planted between them for

## THE COURTS
### Fern Garden

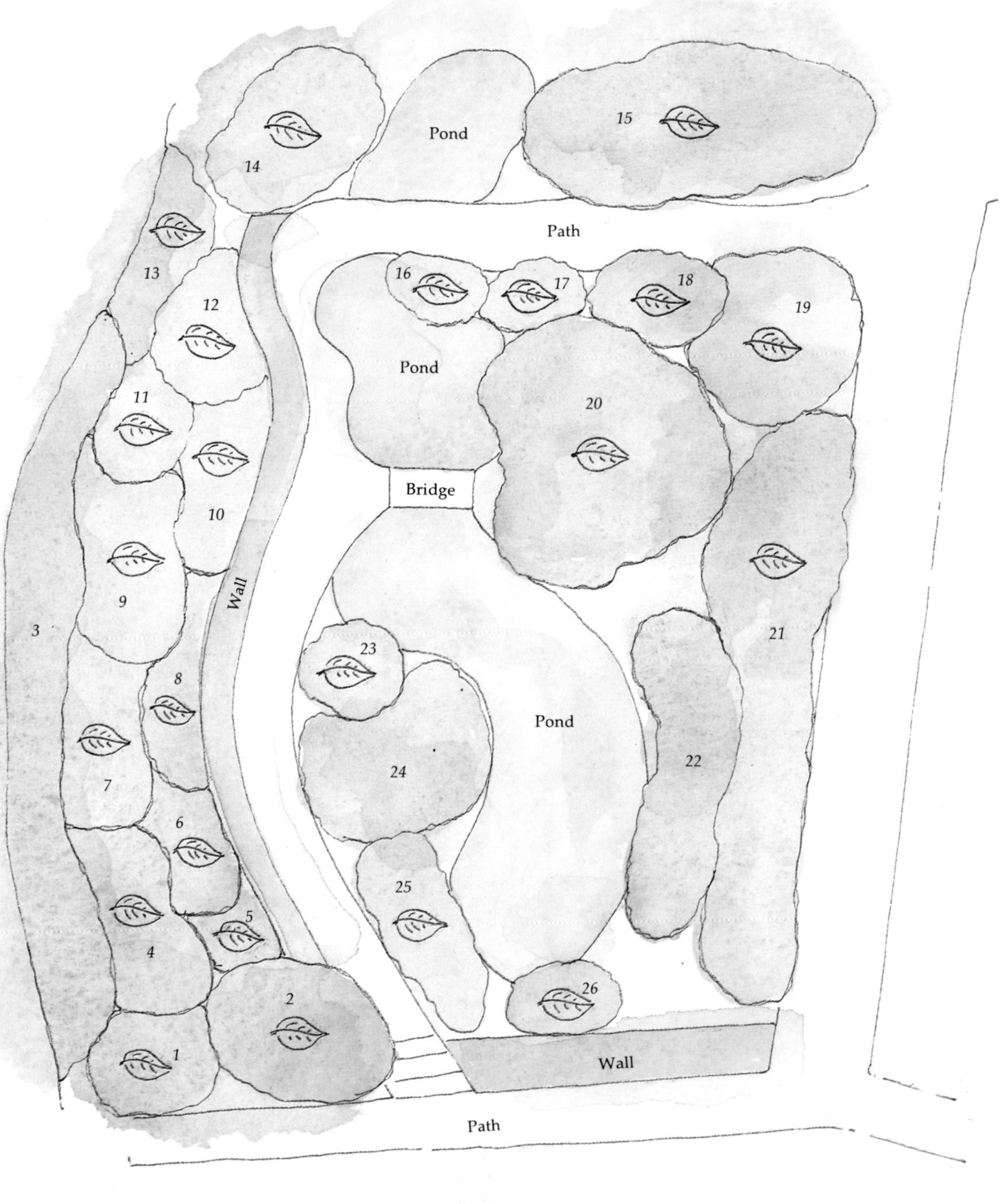

Pond

14

15

Path

N
↓

16

17

18

19

13

12

Pond

11

20

10

Bridge

9

21

8

23

7

Pond

22

6

24

5

25

4

2

26

1

Wall

Path

1. *Taxus baccata*
2. *Buxus sempervirens*
3. *Lonicera nitida*
4. *Dryopteris filix-mas*
5. *Asplenium scolopendrium*
6. Polystichum
7. *Hosta sieboldiana*
8. *Asplenium scolopendrium*
9. *Matteuccia struthiopteris*
10. *Asarum europaeum*
11. *Polystichum setiferum*
12. *Blechnum spicant*
13. *Taxus baccata*
14. *Prunus laurocerasus*
15. *Arundinaria nitida*
16. *Tiarella cordifolia*
17. *Osmunda regalis*
18. *Arundinaria nitida*
19. *Hydrangea quercifolia*
20. *Hosta sieboldiana*
21. *Arundinaria*
22. *Primula florindae*
23. *Tolmiea menziesii*
24. *Primula rosea grandiflora*
25. *Onoclea sensibilis*
26. *Osmunda regalis*

DIMENSIONS: *11m×9.5m (36ft×30ft)*

contrast. *Lonicera nitida*, yew and box provide the rest of the boundary that separates this little place from the seven-acre garden. Pools of *Primula florindae* and *P. rosea grandiflora* are planted close to the pond with a big clump of bold-leaved *Hosta sieboldiana* for contrast. At either end of the pond are stands of the handsome royal fern, *Osmunda regalis*. Where it is happy, this will grow to at least 1.5m/5ft, but it must have

moisture continually at its roots, so is an ideal plant for the waterside. The sterile fronds are light green and elegantly lacy. The fertile fronds are so reduced that they look like brown seed heads. The low-growing sensitive fern, *Onoclea sensibilis*, with broad triangular fronds, is planted near the water's edge together with a patch of *Tolmiea menziesii*, the piggy-back plant.

*The sensitive fern,* Onoclea sensibilis *which rarely grows more than 300mm/1ft high, reflected in a pool of the rock garden at Sizergh.*

On the raised bed are those ferns that need less to drink than osmunda and onoclea. At the back is a fine stand of the shuttlecock fern, *Matteuccia struthiopteris*, which erupts from the ground in late spring. The British native hard fern, *Blechnum spicant*, finds a home here together with the soft shield fern, *Polystichum setiferum*, both of which are evergreen. The common male fern, *Dryopteris filix-mas*, grows at the back of the raised border behind the strap-leaved hart's tongue, *Phyllitis scolopendrium*. Clumps of *Hosta sieboldiana* and *Asarum europaeum* with shining kidney-shaped leaves provide a contrast to the fern fronds. It is a very cool, contemplative, pleasing place to be, and the planting could easily be adapted to a shady courtyard, provided sufficient care was taken to plant in cool, humus-rich soil. Most ferns do best in slightly acid soils, but the hart's tongues (*Phyllitis* cvs.) and the limestone oak fern, *Gymnocarpium robertianum*, favour alkaline soils.

Ferns are not difficult to look after, provided they are planted in the right place. Most need light shade and soil which remains pleasantly moist in summer without getting waterlogged in winter. If you have doubts about drainage, a raised bed such as the one made at The Courts will overcome any difficulties. Coarse grit and humus in the form of leaf-mould, peat or chopped bark should be mixed into the soil, together with a liberal dressing of bonemeal, roughly 135g per square metre or 4oz to every square yard.

The best planting times are the traditional ones of spring and autumn. Ferns need to be kept free of weeds until they are well established. A thick top dressing of peat or leaf-mould in spring will help to keep down weeds and (applied after rain) conserve moisture in the soil. In cold areas, old fern fronds are best left as some protection for the crown during winter. These can then be cut away in spring as the new shoots appear. More bonemeal can be added with the spring mulch.

In mixed plantings, ferns associate well with the smaller rhododendrons and azaleas that enjoy the same slightly acid, moist soil. Acers, too, are natural companions. Solomon's

The common male fern, Dryopteris filix-mas, *the undersides of its fronds heavily beaded with spores.*

seal and some of the shade-loving lilies can be added for variety, as well as *Cyclamen hederifolium* which will help to brighten up the front of the border. In the wild, ferns often seed themselves into shady rock crevices and genera such as *Asplenium* and *Cystopteris* are ideal for planting on the north face of retaining walls or in the risers of stone steps.

Some ferns, such as *Osmunda regalis*, like almost bog

*Soft green foliage of* Osmunda gracilis, *seen here in July, against a contrasting background of grey stone.*

beauty. However, the hart's tongue can adapt to dry conditions, as it has to if it seeds itself into a dry stone wall. As you would expect, in this situation, the fronds are not so lush as those on a plant growing with more moisture. The spleenworts, varieties of *Asplenium*, can also cope with dry conditions.

Although on a scale that few of us could emulate, the Trust's finest collection of ferns is at SIZERGH CASTLE. Hayes of Ambleside laid out a superb rock garden here in 1926 for the castle's owner, Lord Strickland. It covers a quarter of an acre, a masterly assemblage of rocks, conifers, pools, waterfalls and nearly one hundred different varieties of hardy fern. The National Collections of five different genera – *Osmunda*, *Cystopteris*, *Asplenium*, *Phyllitis* and *Dryopteris* – are held here by the Head Gardener, Mr Malcolm Hutcheson. There are bronze and purple-leaved *Osmunda* and at least sixteen species and forms of *Dryopteris*. *Dryopteris wallichiana* has fronds that uncurl like a snake's head, the midribs dark and devious. *Dryopteris erythrosora* has crimson spore cases on the reverse of the fronds. Some ferns such as *Polystichum setiferum setoso-congestum* have thick, hairy midribs, as furry as a rabbit skin.

At Sizergh care is taken to plant ferns with neighbours that have contrasting foliage forms. The shiny, broad-leaved *Lysichiton americanus* sits beside a clump of the royal fern, and a plain carpet of dark-leaved bugle underpins the lacy fronds of the Kashmir male fern.

In the mild climate of the west country, the range of ferns that can be grown is even wider. At TRENGWAINTON a superb clump of *Blechnum tabulare* with broad, arching fronds grows on the left-hand side of the entrance drive. Even the tender Australian tree fern (*Dicksonia antarctica*) will thrive outdoors here; farther north this needs the protection of a cool conservatory. There is a fine planting of them at TATTON PARK in the fern house built by Joseph Paxton in the middle of the nineteenth century. Their arching fronds reach almost to the roof and under them is the elegant *Woodwardia radicans* with agapanthus and *Sophora tetraptera*. Ferns flourish, too, in the

conditions. If there is plenty of moisture available, sun becomes less of a hazard for others; the sensitive fern (*Onoclea sensibilis*) and the shuttlecock fern (*Matteuccia struthiopteris*) will both grow in full sun provided that their feet can be kept permanently damp. If they are not, fronds start to wither. The maidenhair fern (*Adiantum pedatum*) burns very easily: shade is essential for this black-stemmed

*Ferns have been slow to regain the popularity they had in Victorian times, when they were avidly collected. They are ideal plants for cool, shady courtyards such as you find in many town gardens, where their foliage remains strikingly fresh all summer.*

conservatory at FELBRIGG where *Polystichum setiferum divisi-lobum* and the maidenhair fern, *Adiantum pedatum*, partner large specimens of camellia. At PECKOVER HOUSE there is a classic little fern house, no more than a lean-to passage, but perfectly in keeping with the Victorian atmosphere of the garden. Here, ranged in pots on the north-facing shelves, are fine examples of various asparagus ferns, selaginellas (close relatives of ferns), spleenworts and splendidly frilled and crested examples of native ferns gone mad.

## GRASSES AND GRASSLIKE PLANTS

Grasses seem to have less slippery genes than ferns. There is a great variety of them to be grown, but individual species do not show the same tendencies as ferns to erupt into strange and fanciful forms.

It is unfortunate that, as a race, grasses are more often encountered as enemies than as friends. The most familiar battleground is the lawn, where once a week through the summer, the gardener has to take on a polyglot mixture of bents, fescues and ryes and force them into submission. There are also more sporadic skirmishes to be fought against weeds in the borders: annual meadow grass is easily conquered, couch a potentially more subversive foe. There are, however, about 9,000 different kinds of grass in the world and not all of them are bad. Miscanthus, festuca, calamagrostis, and stipa can all be used to great effect in mixed plantings. They come into their own in late summer and early autumn when many herbaceous perennials are beginning to sag at the knees. Even after frost has put a brake on growth, grasses still look handsome with their elegant frozen-fountain outlines and long-lasting seed-heads.

The sedges are not true grasses, nevertheless they provide an excellent choice of varieties for the garden. Mr Peter Hall, Head Gardener, is putting together a collection of them at DUNHAM MASSEY where they seem to thrive in the acid, sandy soil of this shady garden. Several different species are used in the formal beds of the courtyard. *Carex oshimensis* 'Evergold' is not more than 150mm/6in high but makes a

*Tall late flowering plumes of pampas grass,* Cortaderia selloana *silhouetted against the sky at Waddesdon Manor.*

dense clump of narrow leaves, each with a creamy stripe down the middle. It is evergreen and performs best in a cool place, which is not too dry. The colour shows up best out of full sun. In one of the courtyard beds it is partnered by *Hosta lancifolia* and *Primula capitata mooreana*, in another by *Dicentra spectabilis* 'Alba'.

The equally low-growing *Carex fraseri* is planted together with the white-flowered *Pulmonaria* 'Margery Fish' and *Hosta sieboldii*. Bowles's golden grass edges another bed together with the white, willow-leaved gentian and *Epimedium* × *versicolor* 'Sulphureum'. The epimediums enjoy the same conditions as the sedges, and their flat, polished leaves provide a good contrast for the thin, tufty leaves of the sedge.

Unlike the *Carex* species, most of the true grasses like a soil that is light and free-draining with plenty of sun overhead. (On damp soils, the tussocky varieties like *Festuca glauca* have a tendency to rot.) Given these conditions, they are not difficult to look after. If you dig in plenty of manure when you are first planting them, they should not need any more feeding. It is best to cut down dead foliage in March or April before new growth starts. If you want to divide existing clumps, do it in spring or early summer, rather than in autumn. Festucas can be divided every year. If you plant invasive species such as gardeners' garters (*Phalaris arundinacea*) or the creamy-yellow striped *Glyceria maxima* 'Variegata', you will need to keep them in check. Either lift and replant them each year or trench around the clumps severely each autumn, as though you were digging a moat, and throw away any roots and shoots that are outside this *cordon sanitaire*.

Unfortunately, grasses suffer from the same disadvantage as ferns; their proper names feel as comfortable in the mouth as a half-chewed dictionary. Hakonechloa is a case in point. It is a grass that badly needs a name as undaunting as the

*Spiky blue clumps of the grass* Festuca glauca *used with diascias in the rose border at Powis Castle.*

familiar gardeners' garters. *Hakonechloa macra* 'Albo-aurea' a low, tussocky grass from Japan, makes clumps about 300mm/1ft across and as much high. The leaves are quite broad for a grass, and they splay out from the centre of the clump to make a brilliant half-sphere of foliage, yellow with fine green stripes. At COLETON FISHACRE it looks very good with a purple sage and chocolate-scented *Cosmos atrosanguineus* as companions.

At the other end of the scale are the tall grasses that can leap up to 3m/10ft in a season. All these kinds look best in a position where they are not too closely muddled up with their neighbours, but can stand with enough elbow room to show off their natural fine form. Miscanthus is a case in point, either the fine variety *M. sinensis* 'Variegatus', with a thin white stripe down the centre of each leaf, or the more hectically cross-banded 'Zebrinus', striped in yellow across the leaf. One of this family, *Miscanthus* 'Silver Feather', makes a useful scaled-down version of the familiar pampas grass. It has similar plumes of flowers, about 1.8m/6ft high, which will stand until after Christmas.

Where these big grasses do have neighbours, they need to be ones with big, bold leaves for contrast. Acanthus would be good with miscanthus, with hostas or bergenias in the foreground. At DUNHAM MASSEY *Miscanthus sinensis* 'Variegatus' is used with *Aconitum vulparia*, the giant lily *Cardiocrinum giganteum yunnanense* and groups of *Nicotiana affinis*. In another grouping the yellow-banded *Miscanthus sinensis* 'Zebrinus' is used with white Japanese anemones, the huge pinnate leaves of *Aralia racemosa* and a yellow foxglove, *Digitalis grandiflora* 'Dropmore Yellow'.

*Stipa gigantea* is another of the giant grasses that lends itself to dramatic plantings. At OVERBECKS Mr Tony Murdoch uses it with spiky phormiums, the variegated 'Cream Delight' and reddish-leaved 'Bronze Baby'. This particular garden has some brilliant plant associations, *Cortaderia pumila* with *Nicotiana langsdorfii*, foxy-red *Carex buchananii* with the whipcord *Hebe armstrongii* and bronze cordyline. Unfortunately, not all of them can be reproduced in those

## DUNHAM MASSEY
### Courtyard bed

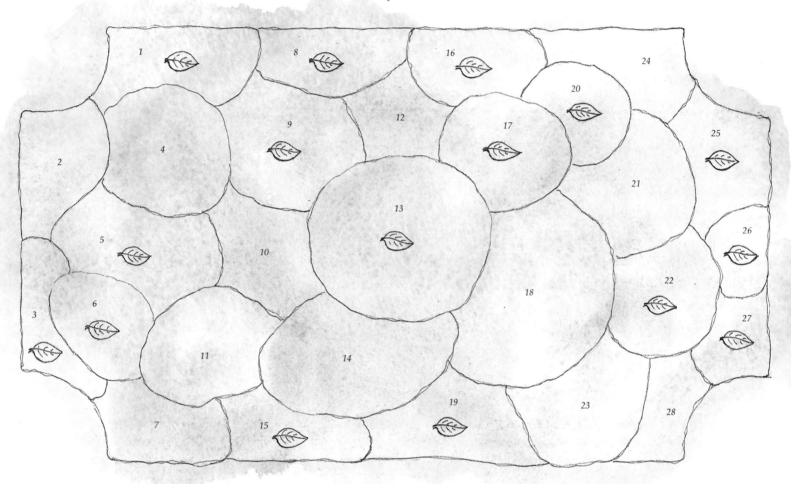

1. *Carex morrowii* 'Evergold'
2. *Primula capitata mooreana*
3. *Vinca minor* 'Aureo-variegata'
4. *Solidago* 'Lemore'
5. *Smilacina racemosa*
6. *Hosta fortunei* 'Marginata Alba'
7. *Primula sikkimensis*

8. *Hosta lancifolia*
9. *Nicotiana sylvestris*
10. *Aconitum* 'Spark's Variety'
11. *Meconopsis* 'Slieve Donard'
12. *Aconitum vulparia*
13. *Eucryphia nymansensis* 'Nymansay'
14. *Astilbe* 'Professor van der Wielen'

15. *Epimedium* × *versicolor* 'Sulphureum'
16. *Alchemilla mollis*
17. *Miscanthus sinensis* 'Variegatus'
18. *Cardiocrinum yunnanense*
19. *Carex elata* 'Aurea'
20. *Polemonium foliosissimum*
21. *Nicotiana affinis*

22. *Kirengeshoma palmata*
23. *Gentiana asclepiadea alba*
24. *Primula florindae*
25. *Pulmonaria* 'Margery Fish'
26. *Carex fraseri*
27. *Hosta sieboldii*
28. *Primula florindae*

DIMENSIONS: *3.9m×6.9m (13ft×23ft)*

↑
N

*A tall bamboo makes a fountain of foliage at Trengwainton. A specimen this size will overwhelm the average garden, but there are plenty of others, not so greedy of space, to choose from in this large and diverse family.*

British gardens which do not benefit from such a sunny climate as that of Overbecks.

For a more fleeting effect, use annual or biennial varieties of grass which can be sown outside in autumn or in spring and can usually be relied on to perpetuate themselves by self-seeding. One of the prettiest is the quaking grass, *Briza maxima*, which has particularly good seed-heads like small woven lockets that tremble on thread-like stems. *Pennisetum villosum* produces soft, feathery plumed heads like woolly cream caterpillars. White hare's tail, *Lagurus ovatus*, has shorter furry heads, equally soft and pliant. All these annual varieties are fairly short, 450-600mm/18-24in high, and so are best used in patches at the front of a mixed border. Their chief interest lies in their flower-heads. The foliage is no more than – well – grassy.

## BAMBOOS

With bamboos, the opposite is true. Flowering is a disaster, leading at worst to the death of the plant and at best to its looking so scruffy and ill that you wish it would die and put you out of your misery. The word 'bamboo' covers three principal genera: *Arundinaria*, *Phyllostachys* and *Sasa*. The last may seem the most promising, as it is the easiest to pronounce, but most of the sasas are fairly invasive and difficult to keep under control in a mixed planting. One of them, *Sasa veitchii*, was William Robinson's favourite bamboo, but he always had a lot of space to play with. It has large, dark green leaves with a pale parchment edging and underground stems that are tougher than a thick-gauge wire.

Some of the dwarf arundinarias are equally dangerous. Beware of *A. pumila* (now to be known as *Pleioblastus humilis*

'Pumilus') and *A. vagans*, whose very naming highlights the problem. These bullies are sometimes advertised as excellent ground cover, which they are as long as you do not want anything else to grow in the garden. The most useful varieties are likely to be the relatively short (1.2m/4ft) *A. variegata* (correctly *Pleioblastus variegatus*) with striped green and white foliage and the taller, graceful *A. murielae* (also known as *Semiarundinaria murielae*). All this jiggering about with names does not help the bamboo's cause one jot. *Arundinaria murielae* is one of the species that Mr Robert Ludman, the Gardener at STANDEN, has used to replant the bamboo garden there after the original species flowered and

died. It is a particularly graceful thing with branches that arch outwards and foliage that is airy and light. The sound of a breeze rustling through bamboo foliage is on its own a good enough reason to plant some.

The odd man out in the bamboo family is the Chilean bamboo *Chusquea culeou*, which can easily grow up to 5.5m/18ft tall. It has very thick canes with densely leafy branches clustered around them. The leaves themselves are small. A big clump of it is used in the streamside planting at DUNHAM MASSEY, where it provides a contrast to the rosemary-leaved willow, *Salix elaeagnos*, spiky phormiums and the big yellow thistle-heads of *Centaurea macrocephala*.

## CATALOGUE OF PLANTS

### Arundinaria
*Evergreen bamboo   Height and spread varies according to species*
The reasonably dwarf variety *A. viridistriata* (now known as *Pleioblastus viridi-striatus*) at 900mm/3ft, is a useful bamboo to work into mixed plantings. The canes are flushed with purple and the leaves are striped with green and rich golden yellow. Provided it is growing in moist soil, it will be happy. You can tidy it up by cutting it down to the ground each spring. A touch of sun will brighten the gold variegation. Even smaller is *A. pygmaea* (now known as *P. pygmaeus*), at most 300mm/1ft high with young shoots pale green, turning to a darker shade as they mature. This is a useful plant to use beside a small pool. Provided they are not allowed to dry out, bamboos also look good in large pots on terraces or in town courtyards. A bamboo needs nothing with it.

### Carex (Sedge)
*Evergreen perennial   Height and spread 150 × 300mm/6 × 12in (varies with type)*
The sedges can bring a wide range of foliage colour into a planting scheme, provided that the

soil is cool and moist. They are ideal for planting by streams and pools. Where quick cover is needed, the slightly invasive *Carex riparia* 'Variegata', leaves almost white with a narrow green margin, would be a useful ally. More subtle is the colouring of *C. buchananii* with leaves of soft terracotta and pinky-copper, curling at the tips. At COLETON FISHACRE *Carex conica* 'Hinokan-sugi' is a star with dark green and cream leaves and thin, buff flower-spikes. Shaggy *Carex oshimensis* 'Evergold' has foliage that looks handsome throughout the winter.

### Festuca (Fescue)
*Ornamental grass   Height and spread 225 × 300mm/9 × 12in*
*Festuca glauca* is the most commonly seen species, a tussocky little grass with narrow, spiny, grey-blue leaves. The flowers are buff. It looks scruffy for a longer period than is ideal but can be improved by combing through with a wire rake. At THE COURTS it is used to make an edging round a semicircular bed. Clumps need to be trimmed over in spring to encourage new growth if this grass is to put on its best performance. The

variety 'Silver Sea' has a better colour than the species. A native of Turkey, *Festuca punctoria* is less common but has better foliage, stiffly spiky. All this family demand good drainage.

### Helictotrichon sempervirens (Blue wheat)
*Ornamental grass   Height and spread 900 × 900mm/3 × 3ft*
This is an elegant cousin of the wheat family, with steely blue leaves and feathery heads of seed in July. It is best seen with some air around it, so that its arching style is not cramped. It is used in the borders at BENINGBROUGH with the heliotrope 'Princess Marina', and with willow gentian at DUNHAM MASSEY. At FELBRIGG it is undercarpeted with a pretty purple viola, perhaps the best combination of all. Dead stems and foliage need to be cleared away in early spring before new growth starts.

### Matteuccia struthiopteris (Shuttlecock fern)
*Deciduous fern   Height and spread 900 × 600mm/3 × 2ft*
These ferns erupt gently in spring to make elegant vase-shaped specimens, upright and bright, light

green until autumn frosts change them to tones of yellow. They are supremely graceful and not difficult if you can provide a home that is moist but not waterlogged, perhaps in the dappled shade under trees. They are at their most beautiful when just emerging, each frond curled like a bishop's crosier. They grow well in the re-created fernery at KINGSTON LACY and in a west-facing border at OVERBECKS, planted in front of an autumn-flowering *Mahonia acanthifolia* with a purple-leaved phormium and the big comfrey *Symphytum grandiflorum* 'Hidcote Blue' for company. Large, simple leaves such as those of veratrum and hosta provide an excellent contrast to the lacy filigree work of this fine fern.

*The shuttlecock fern,* Matteuccia struthiopteris, *with ground covering epimedium.*

### Miscanthus sinensis

*Ornamental grass    Height and spread at least 1.2m × 600mm/4 × 2ft*

A plain, dark hedge of yew will provide a superb background for this fountain of a grass, with finely striped leaves in the variety 'Variegatus', purple-flushed in the sub-species *purpurascens*. Brown-silver plumes of flowers rise up in late summer and the seed-heads will stand until Christmas. It is effectively used in the long double herbaceous borders at BENINGBROUGH, arching over clumps of the dumpy *Campanula glomerata* 'Dahurica' and the brilliant magenta flowers of *Geranium psilostemon*. In another grouping in the same border, it partners white Madonna lilies, *Achillea* 'Moonshine' and the blue cup-shaped flowers of *Campanula persicifolia*. 'Gracillimus' is a faintly variegated, dainty, more diminutive form of the species.

### Ophiopogon planiscapus nigrescens (Lily turf)

*Evergreen perennial    Height and spread 150 × 300mm/6 × 12in*

This is not a true grass, but its similar habit and appearance fits it for the same kind of role in mixed plantings. Black foliage is rare enough to make this an eye-catching plant, so it needs to be used with caution. With purples and reds it can be deeply funereal, though impressive in its way. At POWIS, it is used as ground cover in the formal squares of the vine walk, alternating with pale carpets of *Anthemis marschalliana*, but it is slow to increase. In July, it throws up short flower-spikes, purplish in bud, opening to cream. At COLETON FISHACRE it is used with the pink *Argyranthemum* 'Mary Wootton'.

### Phyllitis scolopendrium (syn. Asplenium s.) (Hart's tongue fern)

*Evergreen fern    Height and spread 450 × 600mm/ 18in × 2ft*

In the west country this is a familiar native fern, choosing cool, damp positions, often on the banks of deep-cut lanes shaded overhead by trees. Unlike the lacy fronds of other ferns, the hart's tongue has solid, strap-like leaves, up to 450mm/18in long. They are slightly crinkled and taper to a fine point. Old foliage is best left on plants over winter and cut down in spring before

*Hart's tongue fern,* Phyllitis scolopendrium, *in the rock garden at Sizergh Castle.*

new fronds unfurl. There are several unusual forms, such as *Phyllitis scolopendrium* 'Ramocristata', with fronds that branch like antlers, each frond finishing in a flat, frilled crest. At TINTINHULL the colour of a yellowish clump of hart's tongue is echoed in the greenish-yellow flowers of euphorbia, both of them set against the dark, cut-leaved bulk of an acanthus.

### Phyllostachys

*Evergreen bamboo    Height and spread 2.4m × 600mm/8 × 2ft*

While more dangerous bamboos have growths that zoom around underground as fast as a tunnelling mole, phyllostachys is reasonably well-mannered and sits primly in a clump, fattening slowly as it ages. For a dramatic dark feature use *P. nigra,* which has canes that eventually darken to a shiny black. *Phyllostachys viridi-glaucescens* has a slightly sickly yellow cast to its leaves. All this family make a brave show through autumn and winter but fall to pieces briefly in spring. We have not the same finesse in placing them as the Japanese, but all bamboos have a natural affinity with water and all benefit from having enough elbow room to show off their graceful lines.

### Polystichum setiferum (Soft shield fern)

*Evergreen fern    Height and spread 450 × 600mm/ 18in × 2ft*

Provided its roots stay moist and cool, the soft shield fern will grow quite happily in full sun, but it is perhaps seen to best advantage under trees where it spreads out to make a swirling Catherine wheel of foliage. Each frond is supported by a furry, pale brown midrib. A thick mulch of leaf-mould in autumn will help to keep the surrounding soil cool in midsummer. About sixteen different varieties grow in the rock garden at SIZERGH, including the wide-spreading *P.s.* 'Divisilobum', drooping fronds sometimes reaching 900mm/3ft in length. *P.s.* 'Divisilobum Iveryanum' is more upright with finely divided and crested fronds. This makes a fine specimen in a cool conservatory.

# FOLIAGE AS GROUND COVER

Ground cover can all too easily be seen as poor-quality contract carpeting. Unrelieved wastelands of hypericum and deserts of periwinkle have given it a bad name, which is a pity because when it is used with a little thought it can be as beautiful as it is useful. If you think of ground cover only as a weedkiller, you will almost certainly get the same deadly effect as if you had used a herbicide. Think of it instead as the bottom layer of a three- or four-tiered planting plan. In this way, well-chosen ground-cover plants should contrast not only with their own neighbours on the ground floor, but also provide a foil for the inhabitants of the upper storeys.

A full-blown star such as the variegated aralia, for instance, will need something rather restrained and elegant under it – epimedium, perhaps, or a colony of the purple-leaved *Viola labradorica*, or a mat of bugle (*Ajuga reptans*). A plain shrub such as philadelphus, uninteresting except when it is in flower, would be a waste of space planted on its own, but the ground can be made to pay rent twice over if you surround the philadelphus with an underskirt of hairy pulmonaria and some clumps of the vivid magenta *Geranium psilostemon*, which will go on flowering after the philadelphus's short season is finished. The pulmonaria's leaves, which grow best when the plant has finished flowering in early spring, will continue to look handsome until the end of October.

Ground-cover plants do not have supernatural powers to

*Alchemilla, hosta and geranium provide low-growing ground cover amongst roses and hypericum in the herbaceous border at Acorn Bank.*

kill weeds, though you might be forgiven for thinking so, given the claims sometimes made for them. Like anything else in your garden, without your intervention, only the fittest will survive. Good, strong, dumpy growers such as hardy geraniums or alchemilla will be able to overcome weeds such as groundsel and annual meadow grass by simply smothering them. A creeping plant such as periwinkle, however, slow to establish and scraggy in growth, will not be able to beat even the simplest weeds for at least several years, until it has made layer upon layer of stems to stop light and air getting through to the earth underneath. Even the heftiest ground cover will be no match for the worst weeds such as bindweed, mare's tail and ground-elder. These you *must* eradicate, probably with herbicides, before you start to plant.

Good ground cover is partly a matter of scale. The thuggish plants often used will colonize yards of ground to destroy scale in all but the largest gardens. They may be planted for quick effect, but short-term convenience will soon be replaced by long-term boredom. Less aggressive plants such as hosta, epimedium or bergenia planted in smaller groups will provide equally weed-proof and attractive ground cover much more suited to the small garden than acres of symphytum or lamiastrum. Hypericum is a coarse horror of a plant and very difficult to eradicate, particularly if it gets its roots down among the stones of a retaining wall or rockery. *Lamiastrum galeobdolon* is another plant that needs a 'Danger' notice stuck on it. In garden centres and nurseries it looks very appealing with its silver-washed leaves. But it is a more determined empire-builder than the Victorian British and, rooting as it goes, a single plant can easily cover ten square metres in a season. As it grows so vigorously, it tends not simply to thread its way politely round neighbours, but go over and through them until they are persuaded, Mafia-style, to give up operations in that particular area.

Fortunately, there are more good plants than bad and, instead of thinking of ground cover as a boring (if serviceable) commodity, think of it instead as a way of increasing the amount of plants and the variety of effects in your garden: not contract carpeting, but a Persian rug of intricate and carefully controlled colour and texture.

By definition, ground-covering plants are low-growing but can differ markedly in their habits of growth. There are clumpers, such as geranium, alchemilla, astrantia, which together make a series of low hills. Too much of that can be soporific. There are creepers, some that root overground as they go (periwinkle, alpine strawberry, bugle), some with running underground roots such as mint, which can be difficult to keep within bounds. With these plants, the individual leaf is less important than the textural effect of the whole mass. Bergenia and arum have large, bold leaves which can be useful to offset the fussy impression given by a mass of small leaves. *Arum italicum marmoratum (A. i. pictum)* is particularly useful in winter. Its arrow-shaped leaves, richly veined in ivory-white, start to unfurl in early autumn and stand until early June. Since the herbaceous geranium's life-cycle is exactly the opposite – it starts up in spring and dies back in autumn – these two planted together will furnish a piece of ground for the whole year.

Bergenias also hold their great, round leaves through the winter. Frost gives them a reddish glow. The flowers of some types can be a particularly virulent pink, bad with daffodils, but the leaves are good against stonework, as at MONTACUTE. They perform better in sun than in shade. They are used, with purple sage, as an underplanting in the iris garden at BARRINGTON COURT, where the big glossy leaves, aptly known as elephants' ears, provide an interesting contrast to the matt green, sword-shaped foliage of the iris. At TRERICE bergenia is used to underplant *Hydrangea quercifolia*, another good combination. The bergenia provides winter interest after the hydrangea has dropped its leaves and in summer offsets the deeply lobed leaves of its neighbour with its own simple, round contours.

## A GROUND-COVERING RIBBON AT ICKWORTH

At ICKWORTH, a long, narrow, highly coloured and ornate Victorian border has been made in front of one of the wings of the house, using only low foliage plants. Because of the way that the land lies, the border can be looked at only from one narrow end. The plants – euphorbia, bergenia, eryngium and tovara – are laid out in four thin continuous lines along the whole length. It is a recreation of the ribbon border, a great favourite with gardeners at the end of the last century, and is an extremely effective way of dealing with a narrow border, particularly one that you view along its length rather than head-on.

None of these plants are weed-smotherers, but were chosen to give maximum contrasts of leaf colour, shape and texture. At the front of the border is a line of *Euphorbia myrsinites*, a low, sprawling spurge with striking glaucous foliage arranged in whorls along the stems – small, rigid overlapping leaflets, rather like the growth of a miniature monkey puzzle tree. The stems, not more than about 300mm/1ft long, snake sinuously along the ground. Some will bear flowers at the extremities in early spring. The flowers (technically, bracts) are a sulphurous greeny-yellow which contrasts well with the steely blue of the leaves. Behind the euphorbia is a row of bergenia, a necessary calm and simple buffer between the spurge and the variegated sea holly, *Eryngium bourgatii*. This grows about 600mm/2ft high, with handsome, curled and prickle-edged leaves, deep green marked out with silver veining. Blue-green thistle-flowers last for two months in summer.

The final ingredient in this unusual foliage border is a row of *Tovara* 'Painter's Palette' which runs along the back. This plant is not to everyone's taste, but if you like coleus, then you will probably like tovara, only quite recently introduced

## *ICKWORTH*
## Ribbon border

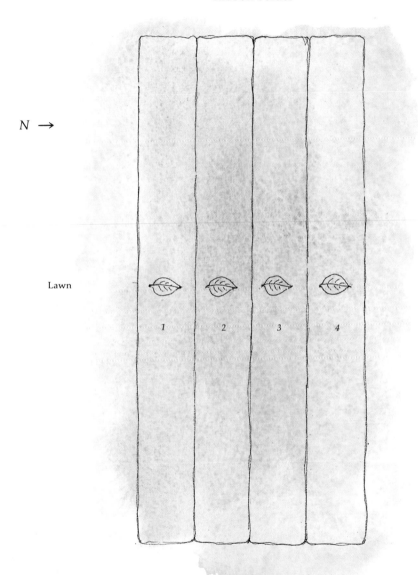

N →

Lawn

House

1. *Euphorbia myrsinites*
2. Bergenia
3. *Eryngium bourgatii*
4. *Tovara* 'Painter's Palette'

DIMENSIONS: *1.8m×39m (6ft×130ft)*

*Golden marjoram and grey-leaved lamb's ear* (Stachys byzantina) *make pools of
foliage colour under apple trees in the old kitchen garden at Powis Castle.*

into this country from the States. It has a coarse habit of growth like a dock and leaves which are green, cream, yellow, red and brown all at once. The red makes a strong V-shaped marking on every leaf and darkens to brown as the leaf ages. Flowers are insignificant, which is just as well: if this plant tried any more tricks, it would explode. The Ickworth border is an excellent example of what can be done with foliage ground cover alone. The formality of its straight ribbons of plants would look well alongside a terrace, or edging a straight garden path. It is obviously important to choose plants that not only provide a degree of contrast, but which also all enjoy the same growing conditions, in this case, good soil and full sun.

## UNDERPLANTING TREES AND SHRUBS

In the old kitchen garden at POWIS CASTLE, ground-cover plants are used in a quite different but equally formal way to make large pools of colour under the ancient apple trees planted either side of the path at the turn of the century by the Countess of Powis. The trees are trained into goblet shapes, and circles under them, about 1.5m/5ft across, are filled with plants of a single type. A gold carpet of marjoram under one tree is set against a grey circle of *Stachys byzantina* under the next. The stachys is split and replanted in mid-October. The dark purple-leaved bugle (*Ajuga reptans* 'Atropurpurea') contrasts with the low silver mounds of *Anthemis biebersteinii* and spiky black *Ophiopogon planiscapus nigrescens*, which are planted under tightly trained trees of 'Arthur Turner' apples. This trick can be adapted to formalize any orchard planting but should be avoided with young, newly planted trees, which need a good area of bare soil round them until they are well established and better equipped to fight for their food and drink.

At OXBURGH the Gardener, Mr Graham Donachie, has cleverly turned some waste ground into a border that is full of interest. A Judas tree (*Cercis siliquastrum*) and a *Viburnum davidii* giving height and substance are underplanted with sarcococca, lamium, bergenia, epimedium and vinca.

Ground-covering foliage plants can be particularly useful in dry shade, where greedier plants will sulk. Ivy, epimedium, the leathery *Euphorbia amygdaloides robbiae* and the triplets, tellima, tiarella and tolmiea will all put up with rather starved homes, such as you generally find underneath trees. If you want them to do more than merely survive, however, you should give them all a thick top dressing of compost in spring, before the ground dries out. This will not only feed the plants, but will help to conserve moisture in the soil.

At ANGLESEY ABBEY clipped ivy is used as a carpet under

*The dramatic bronze-leaved celandine 'Brazen Hussy', discovered as a chance seedling by Christopher Lloyd in the woods behind his garden at Great Dixter, Sussex.*

*Ground cover on a monumental scale at Anglesey Abbey where the common native ivy,* Hedera helix *undercarpets massive yew trees.*

some of the old cedars in the park. This creates a grand if rather sombre effect. At SIZERGH, epimediums are used to underplant *Acer griseum* in the fern garden. The epimediums are an endlessly willing tribe. Gardeners can choose from about thirty different sorts, some evergreen, none growing more than 380mm/15in high, all with handsome leaves like lopsided hearts. Young foliage is often bronze, red or brown-tinged, and gradually turns to green as the season progresses. The leaves colour again in autumn but should be cut back in March before the sprays of small flowers appear. Like the best sort of aunts, epimediums fit in with any company. At PECKOVER HOUSE, *E. × versicolor* is used in a mixed border with hostas, *Kirengeshoma palmata* and groups of astilbes under a large viburnum. In the courtyard garden at COLETON FISHACRE, a completely different effect is created by interplanting epimediums with sedges such as the tall, thin, green and white variegated *Carex riparia* 'Variegata' and Bowles' golden sedge (*Carex elata* 'Aurea').

## EDGING AND INFILLS

Some of the tidier ground-covering plants, such as thrift, pinks, dwarf saxifrage and thyme, make neat edgings to borders or alongside paths. These all need well-drained soil if they are not to rot away in winter. A particularly effective period border has been made at PECKOVER HOUSE using pinks and thrift to divide a long, south-facing border into scallop shapes. Dwarf saxifrage and London pride are used to fill in the shapes along the front of the border, while the scallops themselves are filled with purple and grey shrubs such as *Prunus × cistena* and santolina. The Head Gardener, Mr Paul Underwood, uses a turfing iron down the sides of the thrift in March to keep it shapely; a sharp spade would have the same effect. At ICKWORTH the yellow creeping Jenny (*Lysimachia nummularia* 'Aurea') is used not as an edging but to paint in the spaces between the other plants. The west border is planted with a repeat pattern of *Helleborus orientalis*, romneya, bergenia and dramatic groups of the tall *Euphorbia characias wulfenii*. Around and between them

*PECKOVER*
North border

1. Paul's Himalayan Musk
2. Climbing Rose 'Little White Pet'
3. Climbing Rose 'Blush Noisette'
4. *Iris orientalis*
5. *Crinium × powellii* 'Ellen Bosanquet'
6. *Prunus cistena*
7. *Santolina chamaecyparissus*
8. *Cordyline purpurea*
9. *Kniphofia* 'Strawberries and Cream'
10. Thrift – pink
11. London Pride
12. Mossy Saxifrage
13. *Phlomis fruticosa*
14. *Clematis* 'Comtesse de Bouchaud'

↑
N

DIMENSIONS: *3.6m×15m (12ft×50ft)*

creeps the ground-hugging lysimachia, its bright golden leaves beautifully set off by the dark foliage of the euphorbia and hellebore and by the handsome grey leaves of the romneya. It is a trouble-free plant but does best in a good soil in sun. It would be as well, when planning a border of this sort, to get the upper-storey plants growing strongly before adding the ground cover. Lysimachia grows fast and its eagerness may well dissuade weaker plants from doing *their* best. However, it is a useful plant for softening hard edges of stone and concrete, perhaps by some steps or at the edge of a pond.

Heuchera is not such an accommodating plant. It likes a rich soil and fairly full sun, but the leaves can scorch badly, especially if the sun shines on them when they are wet from watering. If it is not happy, it will make its feelings hideously apparent, but it is worth persevering with, because the foliage can be as sumptuous as a bishop's robe. 'Palace Purple' has leaves that are shallowly lobed, at least 100mm/4in long and wide, deep purple in spring, ageing to a dark purplish-green. They are richly glossy, with pale, matt undersides. Foliage should be cut down to ground level in the autumn and the whole plant thickly mulched. This, together with a handful of some explosive nitrogenous fertilizer in spring, should assuage its appetite.

At POWIS it is used on the top terrace as a foil for the fine Hybrid Musk rose 'Buff Beauty'. This is a very elegant combination, rich bronze-purple under pale buff-apricot. A smaller cousin, *Heuchera versicolor*, is used round another Hybrid Musk rose 'Danaë' with Bowles's black viola for company. Here, too, dark hummocks of heuchera are used with the fine *Argyranthemum* 'Jamaica Primrose', which has deeply cut, ferny foliage (an excellent contrast with the other's fat, rounded leaves) and a long-lasting supply of yellow daisy-flowers.

A different sort of contrast has been created by Gardener Andrew Humphris at THE COURTS, where he has planted heuchera to contrast with the lance-shaped leaves of a blue hosta. At COLETON FISHACRE it partners the strange pineapple tufts of eucomis, itself an arresting foliage plant but doubtfully hardy outside the favoured south-west.

## THE GERANIUMS

By far the most useful single group of ground-covering plants are the herbaceous geraniums, which swam into fashion on the backs of Mr Graham Stuart Thomas's old roses and which have been used to partner them ever since. Collecting them can become a mania and a long drawn out one at that, as about 170 different kinds are available. It is perhaps slightly cheating to talk of them as foliage plants, as they are also valued for their flowers which, depending on

*Low mounds of the useful geranium,* G. macrorrhizum, *here in full bloom on a bank at Standen.*

*The golden-leaved ivy,* Hedera helix 'Buttercup' *is as happy on a vertical plane as
a horizontal, here clothing the trunk of an ornamental cherry,* Prunus serrula.

the type, come out between May and September. The geraniums do have good leaves as well, however; all five-lobed, but some more deeply divided than others. *G. himalayense* has particularly ferny leaves, while those of *G. renardii* are quite different, rounded and sage green in colour, their texture quite rough like sharkskin.

*G. renardii* must have full sun to succeed. Most of the others, such as *G. endressii*, *G. phaeum* and *G. 'Claridge Druce'*, will do perfectly well in some shade. Height varies widely. *G. pratense* is one of the tallest and most vigorous. It easily reaches 900mm/3ft. *G. 'Claridge Druce'* is shorter and has nicely cut, soft foliage with a greyish overlay. The bloody cranesbill, *G. sanguineum*, is a neat, hummocky grower, rarely getting above 300mm/1ft high.

Some, such as *G. endressii* and *G. macrorrhizum*, may be over-enthusiastic colonizers but are easy to heave up and out of the way in autumn. If you trim these geraniums lightly after their first flush of flowers and give them a boost with liquid fertilizer, they will sprout a fine crop of fresh leaves and will usually start flowering again, too. The magenta-flowered *G. psilostemon* is an excellent companion plant for the purple-leaved sage. They are used together at BENINGBROUGH under a tall bush of *Rosa moyesii* 'Geranium'. The bloody cranesbill (*Geranium sanguineum*), which makes a neat hummock of finely cut leaves topped with magenta flowers, is used at THE COURTS around the feet of *Thalictrum speciosissimum*. At MONTACUTE *Geranium* 'Johnson's Blue', one of the ten best plants in the world, is used to offset the deep purple leaves of a cotinus. At WALLINGTON the giant spiky bulk of cardoon is softened with underplantings of *G. pratense*. In a small garden the temptation will be to over-use these geraniums and sacrifice contrasts of shape and texture in the bottom layer of planting. There are worse sins.

*Ground cover plants provide the bottom layer of a three-tiered planting scheme of strong foliage interest at Sizergh Castle.*

## CATALOGUE OF PLANTS

### Ajuga reptans (Bugle)
*Evergreen alpine    Height and spread 100 × 450mm/ 4 × 18in*

In the wild, bugle chooses cool, moist, shady places to grow and it will do best in the same sort of conditions in the garden. It is an effective colonizer, rooting overground as it goes, but should not be allowed to rampage among delicate neighbours. There are plain green, purple or variegated leaved forms, which all have shiny, healthy-looking foliage. 'Burgundy Glow' is particularly handsome, with foliage that is stained pink and purple, each leaf edged with cream. 'Atropurpurea' has highly polished bronze-purple foliage, topped in June with small spires of deep blue flowers. In the woodland garden at TRELISSICK, the cream and grey-green variety 'Variegata' makes a fine companion for the bronzed leaves of *Primula* 'Guinevere'.

### Alchemilla mollis (Lady's mantle)
*Deciduous perennial    Height and spread 300 × 600mm/12 × 24in*

This ranks as one of the most common and useful of all ground coverers. Its only vice is an over-enthusiastic urge to procreate. Be ruthless with self-sown seedlings, or avoid them altogether by cutting the flower-heads before they ripen. The leaves are shallowly lobed and fairly hairy. Their most endearing characteristic is the way that they hold drops of water. It is excellent used *en masse*, as it is round the statue in the fountain of the walled garden at FELBRIGG, or as a soft sea lapping round the craggy leaves of rheum in the streamside border at DUNHAM MASSEY. *A. erythropoda* is a choice plant, smaller and neater than *A. mollis* with leaves the blue side of green.

### Arum italicum marmoratum (A. i. pictum)
*Deciduous tuber    Height and spread 300 × 450mm/ 12 × 18in*

This is an elegant and more refined relative of the native Lords and Ladies or cuckoopint. It grows in the same way, throwing up in early winter furled shoots which unfold into bold arrow-shaped leaves. These die back in early June, leaving an evil-looking spathe, which by September is clustered with brilliant red berries. Whereas the leaves of the wild arum are plain, this variety has superb, glossy, dark green foliage, veined all over in ivory white, except for a narrow plain margin round each leaf. Although a severe frost may make it sag at the knees, it will soon recover. It likes a rich, moist soil in sun or light shade. It looks excellent with the feathery foliage of ferns and astilbe, as in the moat at BLICKLING.

### Euphorbia amygdaloides robbiae (Mrs Robb's bonnet)
*Evergreen perennial    Height and spread 300 × 600mm/12 × 24in*

This spurge is an excellent colonizer for semi-wild areas in the garden but is handsome enough to be used in a border as well. Wherever it goes, it will be most effective in a fairly large clump. It thrives in a wide range of conditions, including deep shade but will appreciate a mulch of compost in the spring. The leaves make dark leathery rosettes and in spring there are heads of lime-green flowers that last most of the summer. It is a very good plain companion for spotty pulmonaria and makes a handsome understorey for some pale shrub such as the variegated cornus. *Galtonia candicans* can be used as a late-summer companion. This spurge also provides a useful anchor for some rather insubstantial shrub such as winter-flowering jasmine. It is not reliable for long-term ground cover and invariably dies out after a few years from its original site although it will thrive in newly colonized adjacent areas.

### Lamium (Dead nettle)
*Semi-evergreen perennial    Height and spread 200 × 600mm/8in × 2ft*

All this family succeed best in light shade and quickly begin to look miserable if the ground dries out. A trim over in spring and a feed with liquid fertilizer will help to keep them in good heart. All the generally planted kinds have leaves splashed with silver to a greater or lesser degree. 'Beacon Silver' is a particularly arresting form with foliage that is entirely silver apart from a thin green margin round each leaf. This has pink flowers in midsummer. 'White Nancy' is a similar heavily variegated cultivar, with a white flower. The mildew that invariably covers 'Beacon Silver' with unsightly magenta blotches does not discolour this form. They are easy to control and make useful mats of colour under old roses, ceanothus, abutilon and viburnum. Plant with clumps of the everlasting *Anaphalis triplinervis* for a pale, misty effect. Try it with blue hostas for something a little more substantial.

### Pulmonaria (Lungwort)
*Deciduous perennial    Height and spread 300 × 450mm/12 × 18in*

All this family are ideal ground-cover plants. They grow strongly and when in full leaf, between April and November, will smother any hopeful annual weeds instantly. The best leaves are those of *P. saccharata* which are up to 300mm/1ft long, dark green, generously marbled and spotted with silver and very rough to the touch. It likes the same conditions as the viola, a cool, rich soil in light shade, but is tolerant of a wide range of homes. The flowers drift between pink and blue and appear in early spring. *Pulmonaria longifolia* has distinctive lance-shaped leaves, which hug the ground more closely than other varieties. There are also forms with leaves entirely of silver such as *P. saccharata argentea* and *P. vallarsae* 'Margery Fish'. The bulky leaves of all this tribe contrast well with the delicate, lacy leaves of dicentra, perhaps *Dicentra formosa alba* as at TINTINHULL, where a variegated ground elder adds the perfect finishing touch to a fine spring group.

### Saxifraga × urbium (London pride)

*Evergreen alpine    Height and spread 300 × 450mm/
12 × 18in*

This is one of the most bomb-proof plants in existence. It is very common but not to be despised on that account, as it is neat, handsome and completely free of problems. Its charm lies in its rosettes of foliage, light green and of a succulent texture. A froth of long-lasting pink flowers held on thin, wiry stems appears in May. (There is a variegated version, but it is not as effective as the plain; it is liverish in tone and the yellow speckles of the leaves do not provide the best background for the flowers.) Use London pride to make a neat edging alongside paths or along the front of a border. It will grow happily in full shade, provided that it is not dust-dry. A close relative *Saxifraga × geum* 'Dentata' has enchanting leaves, cut round as if with pinking shears to make a fine zig-zag edging.

### Tellima grandiflora

*Evergreen perennial    Height and spread 450 ×
450mm/18 × 18in*

Although it sulks in very dry positions, this is a useful plant in light woodland, where it clumps up fast to make handsome mounds of rounded, scalloped leaves, pale green in the standard variety, but flushed with purple and bronze, particularly in winter, in the sub-species *rubra*. The flowers are of the minimalist school, pale green bells, tinged with pink. The bronzy foliage is valuable in winter when so much else has died away. At ICKWORTH the Head Gardener Mr Jan Michalak uses it under plantings of *Cornus alba* 'Elegantissima'. It is equally good under the pale arching branches of *Rubus thibetanus.*

### Vinca (Periwinkle)

*Evergreen sub-shrub    Height and spread at least 100
× 600mm/4in × 2ft*

These take some time to produce effective ground cover and will need a certain amount of hand-weeding until they become established. Mulching with peat or ground bark will help keep down annual weeds. Vincas are fine in shade, but the creamy colouring of the variegated ones will be brighter in good light. *V. major* has the larger leaves and makes clumps of growth that arch up and out and then root as they go; *V. minor* is smaller in leaf and flower, but has a very pretty form 'Argenteo-variegata' with green and white leaves, and another, 'Aurea', which has brilliant gold leaves topped by white flowers in spring. Periwinkles make a neat carpet under the half-standard specimens of tamarisk that line one of the castle walks at DUNSTER.

### Viola labradorica purpurea (Purple-leaved violet)

*Semi-evergreen alpine    Height and spread 150 ×
300mm/6 × 12in*

A damp soil and a shady situation will please this neat, purple-leaved violet which has flowers of pale mauve in April-May. Unfortunately they have no smell. Greenland is its natural home and you should try to give it the same cool growing conditions. It makes a fine foil for snowdrops. For a more startling contrast, plant it with the golden grass *Milium effusum aureum*. At TINTINHULL it grows among grey-leaved plants. In one planting it creeps about under a filigree-leaved *Artemisia*, partnered with pale blue iris and a huge *Euphorbia characias wulfenii*. In another its companions are the neat *Hebe pinguifolia* 'Pagei' and another viola, 'Bowles's Black'.

**Alchemilla mollis** *(lady's mantle) is a clump-forming ground cover plant. It has sprays of bright yellow-green flowers in midsummer.*

# LEAF SHAPES

## BIPINNATE

*Aralia elata*; *Acacia dealbata* (mimosa); *Osmunda regalis* (Royal fern); *Gleditsia triacanthos* (honey locust); *Artemisia abrotanum* (lad's love).

## DIGITATE

*Aesculus hippocastanum* (horse chestnut); *Helleborus orientalis* (Lenten rose).

## LANCEOLATE

*Hosta* 'Thomas Hogg'; *Hosta tardiflora*; *Hydrangea villosa*, *Symphytum uplandicum* (comfrey); *Pulmonaria angustifolia* (lungwort); *Buddleia alternifolia*.

## LINEAR

Iris; *Phormium cookianum* (New Zealand flax); *Hemerocallis* (day lily); Sisyrinchium; Crocosmia; *Yucca filamentosa*.

## OBOVATE

*Cotinus coggygria* (smoke tree); *Sedum spectabile* (ice plant); *Berberis thunbergii*; *Bergenia* 'Abendglut'.

## ORBICULAR

*Cyclamen coum*; *Nymphaea* (water lily); *Bergenia cordifolia*; *Cercis siliquastrum* (Judas tree).

## PALMATE

*Acer palmatum* (Japanese maple); *Rodgersia podophylla*; *Alchemilla mollis*; *Fatsia japonica*; Fig; *Geranium* 'Johnson's Blue'; *Vitis vinifera* (vine).

## PELTATE

*Peltiphyllum peltatum*; *Rodgersia peltatum*; *Tropaeolum majus* (nasturtium).

## PINNATE

*Mahonia japonica*; *Fraxinus excelsior* (ash); *Sorbus aucuparia* (rowan); *Rhus typhina* (stag's horn sumac); *Robinia pseudoacacia* 'Frisia'; *Polystichum falcatum* (Japanese holly fern).

## PINNATIFID

Common ferns such as the male fern *Dryopteris filix-mas*; *Polypodium vulgare* 'Cornubiense'; *Athyrium filix-femina* (lady fern).

## SAGGITATE

*Arum italicum* 'Pictum'; *Zantedeschia aethiopica* (arum lily).

## TRUNCATE

*Liriodendron tulipifera* (tulip tree).

## TRIFOLIATE

*Cytisus battandieri* (Moroccan broom); *Oxalis inops*; *Trifolium repens* (clover); Strawberry; *Choisya ternata* (Mexican orange).

# NATIONAL TRUST GARDENS

**Anglesey Abbey**, Lode, Cambridge, Cambridgeshire
(0223) 811200

**Ascott**, Wing, nr Leighton Buzzard,
Buckinghamshire (0296) 688242

**Ashdown House**, Lambourn, Newbury, Berkshire
(for opening times call NT regional office (0494)
28051)

**Barrington Court**, nr Ilminster, Somerset (0460)
40610/52242

**Beningbrough**, Shipton-by-Beningbrough, York,
Yorkshire (0904) 470715

**Blickling**, Norwich, Norfolk (0263) 733084

**Bodnant**, Tal-y-Cafn, Colwyn Bay, Clwyd, Wales
(0492) 650 460 (during office hours)

**Coleton Fishacre**, Coleton, Kingswear, Dartmouth,
Devon (080 425) 466

**Cotehele**, St Dominick, nr Saltash, Cornwall
(0579) 50434

**The Courts**, Holt, nr Trowbridge, Wiltshire
(0225) 782340

**Dunham Massey**, Altrincham, Cheshire
(061) 941 1025

**Dunster Castle**, Dunster, nr Minehead, Somerset
(0643) 821314

**Felbrigg Hall**, Norwich, Norfolk (026375) 444

**Gawthorpe Hall**, Padiham, nr Burnley, Lancashire
(0282) 78511

**Hardwick Hall**, Doe Lea, Chesterfield, Derbyshire
(0246) 850430

**Hidcote Manor Garden**, Hidcote Bartrim,
nr Chipping Campden, Gloucestershire
(0386) 438 333

**Ickworth**, The Rotunda, Horringer, Bury St
Edmunds, Suffolk (028 488) 270

**Killerton**, Broadclyst, Exeter, Devon (0392) 881345

**Kingston Lacy**, Wimborne Minster, Dorset
(0202) 883402

**Knightshayes Court**, Bolham, Tiverton, Devon
(0884) 254665

**Lytes Cary Manor**, Charlton Mackrell, Somerton,
Somerset (for opening times call NT regional office
(0747) 840224)

**Montacute House**, Montacute, Somerset
(0935) 823289

**Moseley Old Hall**, Moseley Old Hall Lane,
Fordhouses, Wolverhampton, Staffordshire
(0902) 782808

**Nymans**, Handcross, nr Haywards Heath, Sussex
(0444) 400321

**Overbecks**, Sharpitor, Salcombe, Devon
(054 884) 2893

**Oxburgh Hall**, Oxborough, nr King's Lynn, Norfolk
(036 621) 258

**Peckover House**, North Brink, Wisbech,
Cambridgeshire (0945) 583463

**Penrhyn Castle**, Bangor, Gwynedd, Wales
(0248) 353084

**Powis Castle**, Welshpool, Powys, Wales (0938) 4336

**Sissinghurst Castle**, Sissinghurst, nr Cranbrook,
Kent (0580) 712850

**Sizergh Castle**, nr Kendal, Cumbria (053 95) 60070

**Standen**, East Grinstead, Sussex (0342) 23029

**Tatton Park**, Knutsford, Cheshire (0565) 54822

**Tintinhull**, Tintinhull, nr Yeovil, Somerset (for
opening times call NT regional office (0747) 840224)

**Trelissick Garden**, Feock, nr Truro, Cornwall
(0872) 862090

**Trengwainton Garden**, nr Penzance, Cornwall
(0736) 63021

**Trerice**, St Newlyn East, nr Newquay, Cornwall
(0637) 875404

**Wallington**, Cambo, Morpeth, Northumberland
(067074) 283

# SELECTED READING AND LIST OF SUPPLIERS

## BIBLIOGRAPHY

As all cookery writers acknowledge a debt to the seminal works of Elizabeth David, so gardening writers must pay tribute to the writings of Christopher Lloyd, who sets the highest possible standards for all who come after him. His *Foliage Plants* which first appeared in 1973, was published by Viking in a revised edition in 1985, price £10.95.

Other useful books include *The Readers Digest Encyclopaedia of Garden Plants and Flowers* (Readers Digest 1971), *The Hosta Handbook* by Paul Aden (Christopher Helm 1988) and *Foliage Plants* by Ursula Buchan (Cassell/RHS 1988).

## LIST OF SUPPLIERS

**Ann and Roger Bowden**, Cleave House, Sticklepath, Okehampton, Devon EX20 2NN (Hostas only)

**Foliage and Unusual Plants**, The Dingle, Pilsgate, Stamford, Lincs PE9 3HW (No mail order)

**Goldbrook Plants**, Hoxne, Eye, Suffolk IP21 5AN

**Hadspen Garden and Nursery**, Castle Cary, Somerset BA7 7NG (No mail order)

**Hoecroft Plants**, Fosse Lane, Welton, Midsomer Norton, Avon BA3 2UZ

**Hopleys Plants Ltd**, High St, Much Hadham, Herts SG10 6BU

**Jungle Giants**, Morton, Bourne, Lincs PE10 0NW (Bamboos only)

**Ramparts Nurseries**, Hempster Farm, Combe Martin, N. Devon EX34 0NY

**Unusual Plants (Beth Chatto)**, White Barn House, Elmstead Market, Colchester, Essex CO7 7DP

# INDEX

Note: figures in **bold**
*refer to illustrations.*

# ACKNOWLEDGEMENTS

I am most grateful to Penelope Hobhouse who suggested that I should write this book. The text has been greatly improved by her sound editorial judgement. I would also like to thank the staff at the National Trust's Cirencester office, especially Mr John Sales, for much help and guidance. Mr Tony Lord undertook the unenviable task of checking and updating all plant names. His painstaking thoroughness saved me from some nasty gaffes.

Much detailed information came from the gardeners of the various properties I visited. I could not have done this book without the assistance of Mrs Christine Brain (Barrington Court), Mr Chris Braithwaite (Acorn Bank), Mr Peter Hall (Dunham Massey), Mr Andrew Humphris (The Courts), Mr Malcolm Hutcheson (Sizergh), Mr Jan Michalak (Ickworth), Mr Geoffrey Moon (Wallington), Mr Ray Oliver (Grey's Court), Mr Martin Puddle (Bodnant), Mr Charles Simmons (Blickling) and Mr Paul Underwood (Peckover House). Mr Jimmy Hancock, head gardener at Powis Castle and Mr Tony Murdoch at Overbecks were particularly generous with their time.

The staff at Pavilion Books provided unflagging support and my thanks are due to Helen Sudell and Bibi Slimak, my editors and also to Penny David for her thoughtful comments on the text.

My greatest debt is to my husband, Trevor Ware. His good humour and constant encouragement underpin all my endeavours.

## PICTURE ACKNOWLEDGEMENTS

The Publishers wish to thank The National Trust and its photographers for their kind permission to reproduce the following photographs:

**John Bethell**: pp. 14, 58; **Neil Cambell Sharpe**: pp. 8, 11, 15, 17, 19, 21, 24, 25, 31, 34, 35, 36, 39, 42, 43, 44, 46, 50, 55, 56, 59, 81; **Peter Craig**: p. 71; **Nigel Forster**: p. 29; **Jane Gifford**: p. 74; **Phil Nixon**: pp. 12, 65; **Alan North**: p. 18; **Erik Pelham**: pp. 10, 66; **Robert Thrift**: pp. 16, 62, 75, 77, 78, 79, 80, 87; **Mike Williams**: pp. 13, 88.

The Publishers also wish to thank the following photographers for their kind permission to reproduce the photographs listed below:

**Andrew Lawson**: pp. 97, 98; **Tony Lord**; pp. 20, 22, 28, 30, 32, 33, 37, 53, 60, 61, 73, 82, 92, 96, 101; **Tony Murdoch**: pp. 26, 49, 54, 61, 93.